TOOLS FOR

Third Edition

MINDFUL LIVING

Practicing the 4 Step MAC Guide

Kendall Hunt
publishing company

Maria Napoli, Ph.D.

The following interior images are from Shutterstock.com: Facts © Dirk Ercken; Spotlight © Michael D Brown; Explanation point © Palto; Check mark © CoraMax; Floor shapes © Asfia; Yoga posture © Ridkous Mykhailo; Open book page © belkos; Feather © BrAt82; Backpackers © sellingnix; Time faucet © Slavoljub Pantelic; Stopwatch © alexmillos; Emotions signpost © Ryan DeBerardinis; Rocks with flower © sLA vchovr; Orange plate © Markus Gann; Smile in hand © Emin Ozkan; Monster © igor malovic; Captain © Igor Zakowski; Two men at table © Serge SH; Newspaper © iQoncept; Tips for Wellbeing © arka38.

All other shutterstock images contain their credit line.

MAC anagram and 4-Step MAC Guide: courtesy of Maria Napoli

All other line art is courtesy of Valarie Piasticelli

Cover image © Maria Napoli

www.kendallhunt.com
Send all inquiries to:
4050 Westmark Drive
Dubuque, IA 52004-1840

Copyright © 2010, 2011, and 2016 by Maria Napoli

ISBN 978-1-5249-7247-9

Published in the United States of America

C O N T E N T S

Mindfulness has become a buzzword, taking on various meanings such as *flow, being in the zone,* and *living in the now.* Ancient enlightened ones have practiced mindfulness for centuries. Living in the present may have been an easier task before the evolution of technology as we depended upon acute attention for moment-to-moment survival through touching, smelling, and hearing and having an instinct for hunting, gathering food, weather conditions, and predators.

The notion of living mindfully may seem simple; however, integrating the practice into everyday existence can be a challenge in today's modern society. We do not spend days reflecting on a mountaintop, yet noticing the nuances of our lives is worth our time. We lose every moment that passes when we are not paying attention. The big question often asked is, "How can I integrate mindfulness in to my daily life?" *Tools for Mindful Living; Practicing the 4 Step MAC Guide* offers a simple model to guide you in developing your personal signature of mindfulness practice based on your present experiences.

The main message in the mindfulness MAC guide discussed through your workbook is to support you in finding ways *to respond* to rather than *react to* your life encounters, not on a mountaintop, although that would be nice, but in your living room or workplace, walking down the street, or brushing your teeth. When you live mindfully, you can more easily silence the stress reaction and activate the MAC response by mindfully being able to *empathically Acknowledge, intentionally pay Attention to,* and *Accept without judgment* all of your experiences, paving the way to make a choice of letting go patterns of behaving, thinking, and feeling that no longer serve you. Seeing life through the eyes of a child can facilitate moving you into life's experiences with a fresh look.

Life offers many experiences, joys to celebrate, love to cherish, pain and challenges to teach us lessons, and the ordinary and extraordinary goings-on in daily life. Embrace each moment of your life and give yourself the gift of simply noticing them.

Maria Napoli is an associate professor at Arizona Sate University. She has incorporated the practice of mindfulness in research, teaching, training sessions, and presentations at conferences nationally and internationally. She has developed mindfulness programs for elementary school children and undergraduate and graduate students, including an undergraduate and graduate certificate focusing on whole person health with a focus on mindfulness practice. It is her vision to bring mindfulness into education at all levels with the intention of supporting students to perform at their personal best with empathy and focus on quality of life.

Illustrations by Valarie Piacitelli
Photographs, chapter quotes, and poetry by Maria Napoli

ACKNOWLEDGMENTS

As I wrote *Tools for Mindful Living; Practicing the 4 Step MAC Guide* the voices of many people came to mind to which I feel gratitude. First and foremost, the life changes in my students are the energy that drives my vision to bring mindfulness to all levels of education. I am grateful to all of them for allowing me to participate in their transformation as a result of their mindfulness practice. The teachers who comprise a collective energy in bringing mindfulness to our students, Jamie Valderrama, Tamara Rounds, David Shetzen, and Donese Worden and my family who are an inspiration offering encouragement to create a vision to bring mindfulness and wellness to our students. A special thank you to Susan Busatti Giangano for her incredible talent as a musician and song writer and bassist Eric Shetzen for creating the *Simply Mindful Practicing the 4 Step MAC Guide*, an important teaching instrument for developing a mindful practice. Deep gratitude to my teachers Michael Lee and Amrit Desai, who taught me the importance of living in the present, will forever be an imprint in my heart to help students bring nonjudgmental love to everything they think, feel, and experience. A special thanks to the Kendall Hunt Team who have the confidence in publishing Tools For Mindful Living along with the other titles facilitating the practice of mindfulness and quality of life. Thank you to all my readers who are living mindfully as a result of their practice and to the many lives they have touched.

—*Maria Napoli*

Beyond Stress: Strategies for Blissful Living
Maria Napoli

Beyond Stress: Strategies for Blissful Living will offer you the opportunity to tap into your natural resources that may have gone underground, lost quality, or become underutilized as a result of today's fast-paced, convenience-oriented world. Finding the balance of enjoying the benefits of today's conveniences while keeping the innate and precious gifts necessary for the best quality of life; eating foods that nourish; tuning into nature, clean air, soil, and water; embracing relaxation and listening to our instincts is the focus of *Beyond Stress: Strategies for Blissful Living.* The attached DVD guides the reader to practice mindfulness.

Whole Person Health: Mindful Living Across the Lifespan
Maria Napoli and Steven Peterson

Whole Person Health, Mindful Living Across the Lifespan was developed in order to deepen your awareness of areas of your life that are essential to increase overall quality of life. As we mature, we may lose sight of these. Through the lens of mindful living, you will begin to understand how your creativity, playfulness, and humor become less dominant as you grow in age. Each chapter offers opportunities to learn what research and literature has found as well as activities to begin your personal journey. A Mindful Meditation DVD guides the reader to deepen their practice.

Sustainable Living and Mindful Eating
Lisa Schmidt

The practices of Mindfulness and Mindful Eating are introduced as the cornerstones of a sustainable strategy to promote effortless weight management throughout the lifespan. The book's design is to support dietary improvements, which reduces the environmental impacts of food choices through developing an understanding of how behaviors related to food and nutrition can facilitate health balance for individuals and for the environment. A Mindful Meditation CD guides the reader to deepen their practice.

A Family Casebook: Problem Based Learning and Mindful Self Reflection
Maria Napoli

This casebook follows various clinical situations, taking into account the therapist's role and actions beginning with the initial interview and ending with closure. Throughout the book, therapists have the opportunity to mindfully reflect upon their thoughts and feelings as they integrate mindfulness into clinical practice.

PART ONE

Courtesy of Maria Napoli

MINDFULNESS STRAIGHT TALK

Simply stated,
Live in the present.

CHAPTER 1

BE AS YOU ARE

Courtesy of Maria Napoli

I am aware that each moment is completely my experience.
I am aware that all of my thoughts, emotions, and sensations serve me.
I choose awareness.

About Mindfulness

Mindfulness means paying attention to our experiences without internal or external filters. It may seem simple, yet many of our experiences consist of ruminating about the past and thinking about the future. Our experiences are made up of habitual thoughts and emotions, which curtail seeing our lives with a fresh outlook; consequently, we miss what is happening *now*! How would life be different if we got off that rollercoaster and began to live a more mindful life? The never-ending search for satisfaction will end only when we take the time to *Stop, Breathe, and Listen* to our thoughts, emotions, body, and senses. When we are mindful, we are paying attention. That's it! How can living mindfully impact your life?

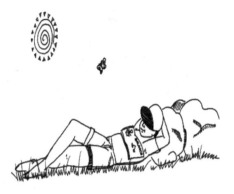

"You can accomplish anything, if you don't put your mind to it."

© CartoonStock.com

Living mindfully opens up the opportunity to be a non-judgmental witness to our present experience. The result is choice. When we pay attention to our experience, we have a *choice* to *do something or do nothing*. Trying out new experiences with the mind of a child, without thinking about the past or future, contributes to the magic of moment-to-moment experiences. We have the privilege of accepting each experience that life grants us, whether or not it elicits positive or negative thoughts and emotions. One thing we can be assured of at all times is that the experience is ours and only we have the power to choose what to do with it.

Your Mindfulness Workbook

This guide was created to offer you a simple tool to apply mindfulness to each and every experience. Its intent is to guide you in applying mindfulness to your entire life. Although we may strive to be present for our experiences, more often than not, we become distracted and do not pay attention. If one area of your life is not in balance, it affects the rest and impacts your overall life harmony. In developing a mindfulness practice, you nurture your curiosity and creativity by noticing and embracing the nuances in your habits and relationships. As you read your workbook and experience the activities, observing your breath, body, senses, emotions, and thoughts, your mindfulness practice

4 Step **MAC** Guide
Mindfully
acknowledge
attention
accept
choose

will expand and develop with your personal signature. As you complete the mindful living activities and the reflection journal at the end of each chapter, you will reflect upon your experience using the Four-Step MAC Guide of 1) empathically acknowledging, 2) intentionally paying attention, 3) accepting without judgment, and 4) willingly choosing your experience.

Learning the four steps is like riding a bike. First, you understand how the mechanism of the bike works. Then you practice. You fall, get back on and have moments of riding smoothly. Ultimately, you ride the bike without even thinking about it. You have integrated how it works, and mastered your own skill of riding your bike as if you have been doing it all your life. The same is true in mastering the Four Step MAC Guide. As you familiarize yourself with the Four Step MAC Guide, you will first become aware of mindfully attending to your experiences. Next, you will practice the steps and finally you will integrate the guide into your daily experiences without thinking about it. When you MAC your experiences and begin to experience a mindful life, you are more focused and better able to make informed decisions.

Let's take a moment and explore a mindless eating and mindful eating experience. We eat every day so this is a good place to start.

Mindless Eating

© Antonio Gravante/Shutterstock.com

Think about your daily routine of eating lunch or dinner. You may prepare fresh food, microwave something, or eat take-out. Before the food actually gets to the table, you might be doing other things instead of focusing on the meal. When you finally get to eat, you may be in a hurry—reading or talking, and not chewing your food well. Some people actually stand or even walk while eating! We become used to this pattern of behavior and are often not aware of what we are doing.

Let us reflect upon your eating a little differently.

Mindful Eating

You have your food before you, regardless of how it is prepared. You arrange a nice setting for yourself at the table, then sit down and view the food with your eyes. Next you smell the food and slowly begin to take small bites. You are aware of the various tastes in your mouth. You chew your food

© Sannikov NikoLA i,/Shutterstock.com

slowly, taking your time until it is almost liquefied (which, by the way, stimulates your digestive enzymes). Continuing to eat slowly, you notice the various experiences you have during the meal, including hunger, thirst, and body temperature. You may also be aware of your breath.

You might be saying to yourself, "Who eats that way anyway? Most people don't have the time to be so focused." This may be true, yet I am proposing a new way of approaching events in your life so that you are fully "in the moment" with each experience you encounter, no matter how small or big. After all, you are the creator and central character in all of your experiences, so why not indulge yourself in them to the fullest?

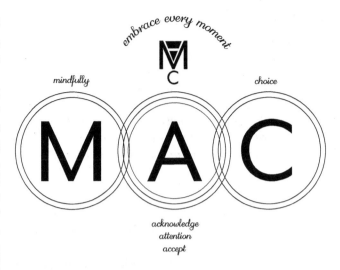

Mindful living is one of the greatest gifts you can give yourself. Each and every activity you mindfully engage in contains the ingredients of acknowledging, paying attention to, accepting without judgment, and choosing your experience with a novel and fresh perspective. Even uncomfortable moments are valuable to us, because they help us grow and make changes that better suit our lives. Repressing and avoiding uncomfortable experiences limit us and take up unnecessary space in our lives. We give those thoughts and emotions, which are attached to those experiences, permission to haunt us over and over again.

Anything from brushing your teeth to creating something spectacular can be experienced fully. When you live mindfully, you are fully engaged in all of your experiences—big, little, dull, and exciting. Why take the shortcut and enjoy only small bites of your life instead of embracing it all?

In theory, this may sound easy, but in our busy lives it can be most difficult to sustain. We are entrenched in our habits of unawareness and being on autopilot. As a result, we lose many magic moments by seeing our world almost as if the past, present, and future were all one experience. In some respects, we have thrown the baby out with the bath water with the advancement of technology, automation, television, Internet, and smart phones that keep us in high gear and moving so fast that those precious moments of our lives escape us.

The most important experiences in our lives occur in our relationships with friends, family, teachers, and other significant people. For the rest of our lives, our development is impacted by the people who raised us. Let's take a moment and reflect upon mindful relationships.

"A study of 'Mindful Restaurant Eating' found that women who met and planned meals weekly at a restaurant lost weight and reduced calorie and fat intake. The participants engaged in weekly weight management topics and two types of mindful eating meditation exercises. One exercise focused on sight, smell and texture of the food and the other focused on awareness of hunger, taste and eating triggers."[1]

Mindful Relationships

From the moment we are born, our perceptions of the world around us are shaped by the interactions of the significant people in our lives. When children develop secure attachments, as adults they are less likely to seek out others to meet their unmet needs. Research has found that children who are raised with caregivers who are attentive and accepting develop enhanced reflective and regulative skills. This ability to pay attention is the road to developing a mindful life.[2] The endless search for "secure attachment" prevents us from accepting our present experience. How, then, as adults do we end this search?

Research has found that when couples are mindful, they are able to deal with conflictual discussion with lower anxiety and anger-hostility.[3] When we accept ourselves without judgment, we are better able to accept others without judgment.

> *"Mindfulness is bringing attention to your present experience without judgment on purpose. It is a state in which you not only have experiences, but you are also able to observe the ongoing contents of your experiences without interference."*[4]

—Maria Napoli

© auremar/Shutterstock.com

The greatest gift we can have when we live mindfully is the capacity for compassion and empathy. When we accept our own joy and suffering, we are better able to accept them in others. Through our acceptance of our experiences, we carve out the path for happiness. How we show up for our experience will determine the outcome. The more time you spend accepting your moment-to-moment experience without judgment, the greater is the field for genuine happiness. When we are not stuck in the past or ruminating about the future, we have more time to enjoy what is happening now. We can embrace the "emptiness" of our minds while we are immersed in whatever experience presents itself. After all, what else is there but this very moment?

The following story about the fisherman and businessman will give you some food for thought about mindfully living in the moment and deciding what is important in life.

The Fisherman and the Businessman

A successful business tycoon was visiting a small island, where he met a local fisherman. He watched the fisherman go out in the morning in his small boat, bringing back his daily catch early in the afternoon. The businessman said to the fisherman, "What will you do with the rest of your day?" The fisherman responded, "I'll have my lunch, play with my children, make love to my wife, and spend some time at the local store playing dominoes with my friends. In the evening, I spend time with my family and then begin my day again." The businessman said, "There are a lot of fish in the water; you can get a bigger boat and catch more fish. You can even buy more boats and ship the fish out to other

© Migel/Shutterstock.com

places and have your own manufacturing company, maybe have a large corporation, go on the stock market and make millions." The fisherman asked, "What would I gain by doing this?" The businessman responded, "You could retire and have a good life, fish in the morning, spend time with your children and wife, and have time to be with your friends."

Thinking about this story, we begin to realize that the best moments in life are our simple enjoyments, not thinking ahead of where we can be, but to be fully present to experience your life as it happens. "When one lives mindfully, the opportunity for self-acceptance increases."[4] Through your journey in your workbook, you will begin to pay attention to the experiences in your life. Let's face it—you are worth it!

Mindful Living

Describe a time when you fully accepted someone unconditionally. Breathe; simply notice.

_____

_____

_____

© Lisa F. Young/Shutterstock.com

Reflect upon a time when you did not listen to your instincts and regretted it afterward.
Breathe; simply notice; describe.

_____

_____

_____

© PathDoc/Shutterstock.com

Can you describe a moment when you felt complete self-acceptance? Take a breath: simply notice.

_____

_____

_____

© esolla/Shutterstock.com

Describe an experience where you felt totally present. Take a breath; simply notice.

_____

_____

_____

HERE AND NOW

© Dirk Ercker/Shutterstock.com

© sunsetman/
Shutterstock.com

Take out the trash. Empty your mind of anything that takes you out of the moment

Describe what gets in your way of being present. Take a breath; simply notice.

_____

_____

_____

_____

"Once nursing students enter institutions of higher learning, faculty should provide caring learning environments that also come replete with enforced rules and responsibilities applicable to both faculty and students. As part of faculty activities to ensure student success, teaching an evidence-based strategy such as mindfulness may facilitate positive student handling of stress and diffusion of anger."[5]

REFERENCES

1. Timmerman, G. M., & Brown, A. (2012). The effect of a mindful restaurant eating intervention on weight management in women. *Journal of Nutrition Education and Behavior, 44,* 22–28.

2. Ryan, R. M., Brown, K. W., & Creswell, J. D. (2003). How integrative is attachment theory? Unpacking the meaning and significance of felt security. *Psychological Inquiry, 14*(1), 177–182.

3. Brown, S., Campbell, K. W., & Rogge, R. D. (2007). The role of mindfulness in romantic relationship satisfaction and responses to relationship stress. *Journal of Family Therapy, 33*(4), 495–496.

4. Napoli, M. (2007). *A Family Casebook: Problem-based learning and mindful self-reflection.* Boston: Pearson/Allan and Bacon.

5. Beddoe, A. E., & Murphy, S. O. (2004). Does mindfulness decreases stress and foster empathy among nursing students? *Journal of Nursing Education, 43*(7), 305–312.

MINDFUL AWARENESS REFLECTION JOURNAL

Choose one mindful experience as you begin your reflection.

Empathically Acknowledge

Describe your experience.

_____

_____

_____

Intentional Attention

Describe what you noticed.

Breath	
Body	
Emotions	
Thoughts	
Senses	

Accept Without Judgment

Describe judgment; acceptance.

_____

_____

_____

Willingly Choose

Intention/willingness; new perspective.

_____

_____

_____

Mindful Mac Meditation

Describe your meditation experiences. What did you learn from your meditation experience?

_____

_____

_____

TODAY'S Insight WOW!

_____

_____

_____

_____

_____

_____

_____

_____

_____

_____

_____

_____

_____

_____

_____

_____

_____

_____

_____

_____

Tips for Wellbeing

- Have Hope
- Accept Yourself
- Exercise
- Practice Mindfulness
- Express Gratitude
- Master Your Environment
- Find Purpose
- Stay Connected
- Be an Optimist

_____

_____

_____

_____

Date: _____   Make Today Count!

FOUR STEP MAC GUIDE

Courtesy of Maria Napoli

Every moment offers a totally new experience.

See With the Wonder of a Child

See the sweetness children have!
Their voices have purity;
Their innocence no purpose.
They are not afraid that someone will
  think they are foolish.
It doesn't matter to them.
A child plays for the sake of play.
Enchanted by the moment,
The timeless time, the eternal now.
There is no purpose in the play;
Nothing to change, nothing to attain.
All that surrounds children is a source of wonder.
Walking, moving, and looking with amazement in their eyes.
A child's eyes are ever empty.
Like a mirror, reflecting
Only what is there.
All is mysterious, surprising, fresh and new.
We have forgotten now, but one day we walked
Our eyes wide with wonder and feeling.
"What's this? What's that? I never saw it before!"
When we are like a child, we experience life,
With freshness, amazement,
And emptiness in our eyes.
Then life itself with all its mystery
Will fulfill our deepest longings.

—Maria Napoli

FOUR STEP MAC GUIDE

1. Empathically acknowledge experience just as it is—Breathe

2. Intentionally pay attention to instincts body, thoughts, senses, and emotions—Breathe

3. Accept experience without judgment or expectations—Breathe

4. Choose how you show up for your experience—Breathe

Empathic Acknowledgment

We are having experiences every moment of our lives. When those experiences are uncomfortable, we may want to wish them away. We may rationalize, deny, repress, or avoid what has occurred, yet the emotions attached to that experience remain, only to rear their heads at another unexpected time. Taking a moment to breathe and empathically acknowledge our experience, offers us the gift of being a more objective witness to the experience. Allowing ourselves to empathically acknowledge not only the core elements of our experience, but also the nuances can be invigorating.

Acknowledging our experience just as it is without trying to change anything is the first step toward mindfulness. It is what it is; nothing more, nothing less. Empathic acknowledgment of our own and other's experiences can increase our ability to feel connected to the emotions attached to those experiences. Theorists note that empathy is the very basis of all human interaction,[1] and when we are empathetic, we enter the private, perceptual world of the other.[2] According to H. Spiro, "When families and therapists are able to focus on one another and share their thoughts without being distracted, they are able to put themselves in one another's shoes and can be more easily available to regulate emotions and accept their differences."[3] Empathic listening is diminished when a person is unable to focus on what's happening in that moment. Taking the time to acknowledge one another face-to-face occurs less frequently and can result in negative thinking and emotions such as blame, anger, and resentment. Holding onto to those feelings ultimately influences future experiences. When you are able to "put yourself in another's shoes," you open yourself to your own pain with acceptance versus rejection and demonstrate a heartfelt tenderness toward yourself and others.

Let's follow the story of Nancy and Jose, who have been childhood friends for many years. They are about to enter college. Nancy is an artist and Jose is an engineering student. They planned to attend the same college and continue their friendship while sharing new experiences. Jose was accepted to a top-tier college for engineering with a full scholarship and decided to take the offer. Nancy, on the other hand, decided to attend their original-choice college. She was upset and felt rejected by Jose for changing their life-long plans and avoided seeing and calling him.

If Nancy acknowledged that she was upset she might not have felt the need to avoid Jose. She might also have been better able to understand Jose's situation and notice how he was feeling. As a result, she might not have felt rejected. Furthermore, if Nancy allowed herself to experience the same situation as an observer of both herself and Jose, she would be more likely to empathically acknowledge the situation and maybe even feel Jose's joy.

This story is simple yet powerful. When we can empathically recognize each other's pain and joy, we are more likely to experience intimacy in our relationships.

Couples who are mindful were found to be better able to manage their emotions, resulting in increased empathy and experiencing greater satisfaction in health, stability, affection, and inter-partner harmony.[4]

Mindful Living

Place yourself in the shoes of someone with whom you are having a difficult time. Describe the experience.

_____

_____

_____

_____

_____

A study of graduate students who participated in a course that focused on enhancing self-care and professional development and practiced formal and informal mindfulness strategies significantly increased their use of mindfulness in acting with awareness, observing, and accepting without judgment.[5]

Think of an experience with someone when you held onto a past experience, felt stuck, or worried about the outcome or expectation of the current situation. Reflect upon the situation with that person. Do *not* empathically acknowledge the experience.

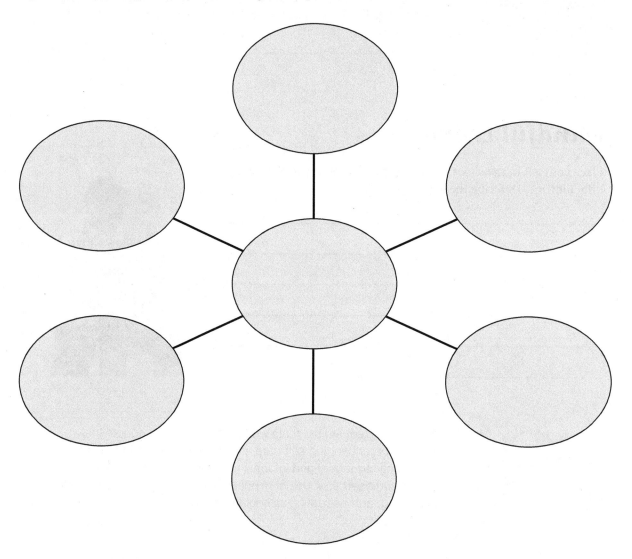

(Place the *name* of the person in the center circle and your *experience, feelings, and thoughts* in the surrounding circles)

© auremar/Shutterstock.com

Empathically revisit that same situation. Reflect upon how the situation with that person might have been different.

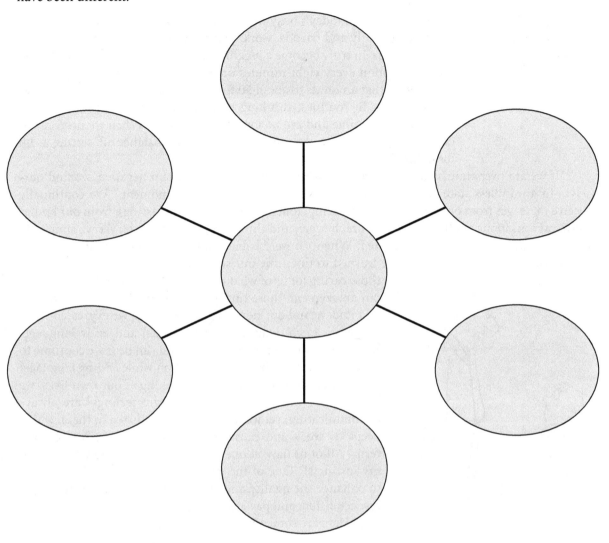

(Place the *name* of the person in the center circle and your *experience, feelings, and thoughts* in the surrounding circles)

Intentional Attention

Paying attention in today's busy world can be a challenge. Balancing priorities among family and friends, work, personal, health, and intellectual and spiritual time can truly become a juggling act. We experience approximately one interruption every eight minutes or six to seven per hour. In an eight-hour period that amounts to about 50 to 60 interruptions a day.[6] Sometimes we are caught in routines, thinking patterns, and ways of behaving that served us at one time and are no longer useful today. When we neglect any one area—never mind two or three—we throw our balance off, setting us up for failure or stress.

If we are overstimulated and overloaded with thoughts, many of them negative, we find ourselves in a mindless state of being unaware of "what's happening in the moment." We continually receive messages from our senses (hearing, seeing, touching, smelling, and tasting); from our bodies (physical sensations and body temperature, hunger, and thirst); and our instincts, yet we simply do not notice what is being communicated. When we were babies, our ability to communicate without language was quite effective. We learned to fine-tune our senses and body language to inform those caring for us of what we needed, when, and how much. To our amazement, those caring for us learned to pay attention to and understand our nonverbal messages as we expressed them in sound, pitch, length of cries, grunts, and body language. Imagine how intentional our attention can be if we continue to develop our nonverbal communication while adding language!

When we stop and observe, looking at our own lives, we begin to see that our instincts and "gut feelings" are always communicating, yet we frequently do not listen to them, which keeps us stuck and causes us to resort to the same old patterns. All of us have at one time said, "If I had only listened to my instincts!" One of the greatest gifts you can give yourself to enhance the quality and enjoyment in your life is to deeply respect, listen, and pay attention to yourself.

Here are some tips to help you do this.

© CartoonStock.com

"Always use your head, follow your heart and go with your gut feeling."

Results of mindfulness training for mothers and their children with attention-deficit/hyperactivity disorder found that children were more compliant when their mother received mindfulness training. Compliance further increased when the children also received mindfulness training.[7]

Mindful Living

Choose one activity today and allow yourself to pay attention to each and every aspect of that experience. Describe. Take a breath. Simply notice.

_____

_____

_____

_____

Each day, choose one of your senses to focus on and describe the experience. Take a breath. Simply notice.

_____

_____

_____

_____

Researchers asked students who were watching a video to count the number of times groups of people passed a basketball to one another. More than one third of the students did not notice that a person in a gorilla suit walked through the scene; in fact, the person in the gorilla suit even stopped to pound on its breast.[8]

Tips to Develop Intentional Attention

- Do one task at a time.
- Keep a realistic short-term list of what you want to accomplish now.
- Listen to your instincts; your gut knows.
- Take long, slow breaths throughout the day for centering and energy boosts.
- Bring awareness to your senses.

Mindful Living

What intentions have you set regarding paying more attention to your experiences?

_____

_____

_____

_____

What steps are you willing to take to help increase your ability to pay attention?

_____

_____

_____

_____

Mindfulness-based cognitive therapy for a child is a good choice of treatment for children because it can help reduce internalizing and externalizing symptoms.[9]

Nonjudgmental Acceptance

Attitude is everything. Too often we are locked into hours of "should and have to" and become stuck in the past or ruminate about the future, which prevents us from embracing the moment. We are often our own worst enemy, placing pressure on ourselves to do better, make more money, please others more, and even judge ourselves relentlessly. Remember, these are lessons, not mistakes. We are all perfect in our imperfections. Letting go of judgments of others and ourselves is probably the most difficult step in living mindfully because we hold onto to these negative beliefs about others and ourselves. We judge our actions, thoughts, and behaviors; we live in yesterday and worry about tomorrow. When we let go of judgments, we can add years of joy and quality to our lives. Some say that time is money; once we lose it and use it up it's gone; we cannot go back and retrieve those ;moments that were drowned in negativity.

This story of John and Ann illustrates the point.

John recently married Ann. He was used to eating breakfast alone, usually coffee and a cookie, and waiting until the last minute to get ready for work. Ann, on the other hand, felt that eating a nutritious breakfast was an important meal that offered her the fuel she needed to begin her day. One morning, John decided to get up 15 minutes earlier and sit with Ann for a nutritious breakfast instead of running out the door at the last minute. After doing so, he realized that he had more energy and did not reach for his daily mid-morning doughnut and coffee. John accepted his experience without judgment. He saw that getting up was not deprivation but rather an enjoyment and surprisingly satisfying. He was able to eat a nutritious meal, eliminate the desire for the mid-morning sugar rush, and spend time with Ann planning the day's events.

A mindfulness communication program studied burnout, empathy, and attitudes with primary care physicians and found improvements in short-term and sustained well-being and attitudes associated with patient-centered care following participation in the mindful communication program.[10]

It is not easy to keep a positive, open, and non-judgmental attitude in a world that is filled with violence, hunger, pollution and greed. We cannot solve the world's problems, yet we can begin with ourselves to make a difference. To maintain harmony in our lives, we sometimes need guides to remind us to keep it simple. Use the following guides without judgment to help you develop the opportunities for personal self-reflection and unfold the unknown on your daily journey through life.

© sLA vchovr/Shutterstock, Inc.

Attitudes Toward Others

- Embrace compassion and sensitivity toward others.
- Embrace your truth and loving communication.
- Embrace moderation in all things.

Attitudes Toward Yourself

- Embrace keeping a clear mind.
- Embrace gratitude and joyfulness.
- Embrace healthy goals.
- Embrace learning, diversity, and self-reflection.
- Embrace the new and novel challenges in life.

- Embrace daily practice of movement.
- Embrace a full-embodied breath.
- Embrace mindfulness and what's happening now.
- Embrace "paying attention" to one thing at a time.
- Embrace integrating all the ingredients that color your experience.

Having expectations about another can lead to rejection and a judgmental attitude. Being mindful may decrease the tendency to take on another's negative emotions.[11] When one is mindful, there is a willingness to accept emotions and actively experience the bodily sensations, emotions, thoughts, and memories attached to them—not to control or minimize them.[12] Social Worker C. Kessen writes, "When families are mindful they can experience each other in new ways, thus moving away from routine and boredom and fixed ways of viewing their relationship with family members, and develop new and exciting ways to be in the relationships."[13] When we approach our experiences without expectation, we are more likely to accept the experience without judgment. When we eliminate judgment, we can stop the mindless monster that criticizes and perpetuates negative thinking and behavior that keep us stuck in old thinking and behavior patterns.

Researchers have found that therapists who practice mindful meditation experience increased empathy and compassion their clients.[14]

Mindful Living

At the end of this chapter, write in your Mindful Journal.

For one week, bring your attention to judging and critical thinking, behavior, and emotions. Take some time to journal about those experiences. Accept your awareness of yourself; simply notice what feelings arise following your reflection.

Elementary school students participated in a 24-week mindfulness program where breath work, body scan, movement, and sensorimotor awareness activities were practiced during physical education classes. Results showed that students who participated in the mindfulness training significantly increased selective attention and reduced test anxiety compared to the control group who did not receive the mindfulness practice activities.[15]

Willing Choose

When you make a decision while attending to your experiences with a fresh look, it can change your life. We all want to change thinking, behavior, and emotions that no longer serve us, yet we often remain stuck in the familiar. Experiencing events from a new perspective is pivotal for creating change. Change can be fun and exhilarating, and individuals who are mindful may feel less threatened by it.[16] Choosing to move forward is the wind that drives the choice into action. Most important, when exploring a method of executing an action plan, take time to breathe and acknowledge, pay attention to, and accept the experience. We can thus set an intention for choosing what action to launch. Desire and willingness often ride the same fence, yet it is our willingness to choose that will bring about change.

When you consciously make a choice, change occurs. You can then turn inward to see who you are and who you can become. A key element to moving forward is forgiving others and ourselves. The willingness to forgive and be forgiven was found to be one of ten positive elements in couples married for more than 20 years.[17] Forgiveness helps one to accept the pain related to the situation, making one less likely to react, better able understand their own suffering, and more likely to communicate that experience to the person involved in the event.[18] "When individuals are mindful they are able to witness their moods and triggers, hence, gaining insight regarding the connections between situations, thoughts and emotions."[19] Making a decision to choose and taking specific actions toward implementing that choice are the benefits of applying mindfulness to situations. Knowing that we are all perfect in our imperfections as humans is essential. Letting go of expectations of others and ourselves while embracing the experiences that have colored our lives is an impetus to move forward.

© Ohn Mar/Shutterstock.com

Keep in mind that change opens up a new space in our lives. This can be viewed as comforting or challenging. As we have discussed previously, when we are mindless and stuck in old behaviors that are uncomfortable, they nevertheless provide familiarity. When we are mindful, we are able to experience the newness of experiences and view those experiences from many perspectives. Opening the door to change liberates us from the past. Living a mindful life facilitates making decisions and taking action to create change.

© KreativKolors/Shutterstock.com

Mindful Living

Take a moment to reflect on a behavior, thinking, or emotion that keep you stuck. Allow yourself to be open to the possibility of moving out of that space. What are you willing to do?

Decision

_____

_____

_____

Action

_____

_____

_____

Change

_____

_____

_____

REFERENCES

1. Kohut, H. (1959). Introspection, empathy, and psychoanalysis. *Journal of the American Psychoanalysis Association, 7,* 459–483.

2. Rogers, C. R. (1980). *A way of being.* Boston: Houghton Mifflin.

3. Spiro, H. (1992). What is empathy and can it be taught? *Annals of Internal Medicine, 116*(10), 843–846.

4. Wachs, K., & Cordova, J. V. (2007). Mindful relating: Exploring mindfulness and emotion repertoires in intimate relationships. *Journal of Marital and Family Therapy, 33*(4), 464–481.

5. Napoli, M., & Bonifas, R. (2011). From theory toward empathic self care: Creating a mindful classroom for social work students. *Social Work Education: The International Journal Social Work Education, 30*(6), 635–549.

6. Westmore, D. (2000). The juggling act. *Journal of Training and Development, 54*(9), 67–69.

7. Singh, N. N., Lancioni, G. E., Winton, A. S. W., Singh, J., Singh, A. N., Adkins, A., D., & Whaler, R. G. (2010). Mindfulness training for parents and their children with ADHD increases the children's compliance. *Journal of Child and Family Studies, 19,* 157–166.

8. Simons, D., & Chabris, C. (2004). Gorillas in our midst. *Perception, 28,* 1059.

9. Lee, J., Semple, R. J., Dinelia, R., & Miller, L. (2008). Mindfulness based cognitive therapy for children: Results of a pilot study. *Journal of Cognitive Psychotherapy, 22*(1), 15–28.

10. Krasner, M. S., Epstein, R. M., Beckman, H., Suchman, A. L., Chapman, B., Mooney, C. J., & Quill, T. E. (2009). Association of an educational program in mindful communication with burnout, empathy, and attitudes among primary care physicians. *JAMA, 302*(12), 1284–1293.

11. Wright, S., Day, A., & Howells, K. (2009). Mindfulness and the treatment of anger problems. *Aggression and Violent Behavior, 14*(5) 396–401.

12. Kessen, C. (2009). Living fully: Mindfulness practices for everyday life. In S. F. Hick (Ed.), *Mindfulness and Social Work* (pp. 31–43). Chicago, IL: Lyceum Books, Inc.

13. Napoli, M. (2011). React or respond: A guide to apply mindfulness for families and therapists *Families in Society, 92,* 28–32.

14. Davis, D. M. & Hayes, J. A. (2011) What are the benefits of mindfulness? A practice review of psychotherapy-related research. *Psychotherapy 48* (2), 198–208.

15. Napoli, M., Krech, P., & Holley, L. (2005). Mindfulness training for elementary school students: The attention academy. *Journal of Applied School Psychology, 21,* 99–125.

16. Burpee, L. C., & Langer, E. J. (2005). Mindfulness and marital satisfaction. *Journal of Adult Development, 12*(1), 43–51.

17. Lawler-Row, K. A., Karremans, J. C., Scott, C., Edlie-Matityahou, M., & Edwards, L. (2008). Forgiveness, physiological reactivity and health: The role of anger. *International Journal of Psychophysiology, 68,* 51–58.

18. Young, M. A. (2004). Healthy relationships: Where's the research? *The Family Journal: Counseling and Therapy for Couples and Families, 12*(2), 159–162.

19. Burpee, L. C., & Langer, E. J. (2005). Mindfulness and marital satisfaction, *Journal of Adult Development, 12*(1), 43–51.

MINDFUL AWARENESS REFLECTION JOURNAL

Choose one mindful experience as you begin your reflection.

Empathically Acknowledge

Describe your experience.

_____

_____

_____

Intentional Attention

Describe what you noticed.

Breath
Body
Emotions
Thoughts
Senses

Accept Without Judgment

Describe judgment; acceptance.

_____

_____

_____

Willingly Choose

Intention/willingness; new perspective.

_____

_____

_____

Mindful Mac Meditation

Describe your meditation experiences. What did you learn from your meditation experience?

_____

_____

_____

Mindful Daily Journal

TODAY'S Insight WOW!

_____
_____
_____
_____
_____
_____
_____
_____
_____
_____
_____
_____
_____
_____
_____
_____
_____
_____
_____
_____
_____
_____

Tips for Wellbeing

- Have Hope
- Accept Yourself
- Exercise
- Practice Mindfulness
- Express Gratitude
- Master Your Environment
- Find Purpose
- Stay Connected
- Be an Optimist

_____
_____
_____
_____

Date: _____   Make Today Count!

CHAPTER 3

BECOMING STRESS-LESS

Courtesy of Maria Napoli

What you do with stress will determine how it affects your life.

Practicing mindfulness can increase our propensity to manage stress more effectively.[1] When we acknowledge, pay attention to, and accept our experiences without judgment, the doors open to allow us to choose the impact of our experiences. We can choose to react or respond. Whatever we choose will dictate the outcome of the stressor. There is a lot of talk about the damaging effects of stress. It is true that stress can have a devastating effect upon our lives emotionally, physically, professionally, psychologically, and environmentally. The inevitable remains—change—and major change in particular often cause stress. The fact is the effect change has upon us depends upon how we deal with that change or, for that matter, any situation that we identify as stressful. This sheds new light on the concept of managing stress. If someone were to ask you, "Would you like to function at your optimum capacity?" chances are you would say, "Of course."

© Maxisport/Shutterstock.com

Having the desire and even the motivation to be at your personal best are often not enough to achieve your peak performance. It is your willingness to do what is necessary that brings out your best! We now know that our experiences can change brain structure. The term neuroplasticity is used to describe this neural connection change in response to our experiences. A. Rogers writes, "Neuroplasticity changes not only neural structural alterations, but they are accompanied by changes in the brain function, mental experience (such as feelings and emotional balance), and bodily states (such as a response to stress and immune functions)."[2]

A great example of neuroplasticity occurs when we enter a state known as "flow." This occurs when there is no distinction between mind and body, no tension between thinking, feeling or doing and thus no working against yourself.[3] Athletes, musicians and dancers strive for the experience of "being in the zone" or flow. This is a moment when nothing exists except the experience, whether it is the swing, the jump, or the perfectly synchronized sound of the violin. It's all the same: body, mind, and energy are in perfect harmony.

Close your eyes, take a breath, and see if you can remember a time in your life when you were mindfully present and experienced that perfect harmony of being in the zone.

Fight or Flight? Or Go With the Flow You Choose

In today's busy world, where many areas of our lives are on overload, we often react to daily events as if they were a life or death situation. Road rage, high anxiety at work and home, overreacting to disappointment, and unrealistic expectations of self and others all contribute to wearing down our immune system from the activation of the fight-or-flight response. Our bodies are hardwired to respond immediately when they receive a message that we need help. When our stress response is activated, our body directs energy where it is needed. Essential bodily

4 Step **MAC** Guide

Mindfully

acknowledge

attention

accept

choose

functions such as blood pressure, breathing, and heart rate accelerate, and nonessential bodily functions such as digestion and the immune system are temporarily slowed down. Our immune system is essentially turned off and is thus unable to be called to battle to deal with the results of the damage caused by stress. Thus, when we need our immune system, for example to fight off colds or fever, the reserve is empty. What can be done to prevent activating the fight-or-flight response when it is not an actual emergency so that we have the reserve during those critical times? Let's see what happens to our bodies during stress.

How Your Body Deals With Stress

The *limbic system* is the main area of the mammalian brain that deals with stress. It includes the hypothalamus, the hippocampus, and the amygdala, often called the emotional brain because it is thought to be related to forming our memories. The moment your body perceives danger, your limbic system quickly secretes the stress hormone *cortisol* and responds via your autonomic nervous system through the endocrine glands that regulate metabolism. During stress, the body needs an increase in metabolism to deal with a potential threat thus going into fight or flight.

The *sympathetic nervous system (SNS)* is part of the autonomic nervous system, which also includes the parasympathetic system and enteric nervous system. The job of the SNS is to maintain the body's state of balance through homeostasis as well as mobilize the body's resources into the fight-or-flight response when it experiences stress. When the SNS deems that fight-or-flight is appropriate due to a real or perceived threat, it activates the physiological functions necessary for survival such as increased heart rate, hormone release and heightened senses while decreasing those functions not critical for immediate survival such as digestion and the immune system.

Anti to the sympathetic nervous system is the parasympathetic nervous system (PNS) that regulates rest and digestion, ensuring that the digestive and immune systems are fully working to guarantee adequate absorption of nutrients, restful sleep, and protection against disease. Together, these two critical systems make up the soldiers that ensure equilibrium within the body, by making adjustments whenever something disturbs this balance.

The *endocrine system* consists of ductless glands that pump hormones into the body to support human development, reproduction, and balance. The endocrine system teams up with the nervous system to keep a check on the amount of hormones that are released before sending them into the circulatory system. When you experience chronic stress, the hormones produced by these glands sit in the brain for long periods of time and can have a harmful effect. The area of the brain that is most affected is the hippocampus, which is the part of the brain that we need for remembering and learning. In order to restore memory and learning, the PNS needs to check in for balance, yet it is unable to do so when the body is flooded with stress hormones such as cortisol.

The *immune system* has one of the most important functions because it is the body's defense against illness and disease and acts by identifying and

fighting off bacteria. When the immune system is called upon to deal with stress, its ability to fight off illness and disease is compromised. Chronic stress can exhaust the immune system, leaving the body defenseless against pathogens that may invade the body as well as compromising the body's internal ability to maintain health.

As you can see, the body is an efficient machine that is prepared to protect us in any situation that threatens our well-being. The key is to give the body the opportunity to do its job by living a mindful life. You cannot avoid stress, yet you can develop a large arsenal of tools to help you deal with any situation that challenges homeostasis. You are deserving of having good health in your life and mindfulness is the ticket for attaining that gift. Note below and see if you are a reactor or responder to stress.

Mindless Stress Reaction

- React when you are angry.
- React when people do not meet your expectations.
- React when things do not go your way.
- React to negative thoughts.
- React when you feel fear or rejected.

© MaxFX/Shutterstock.com

When we respond to our experiences, we are better able to regulate emotions and behavior. Respond offers the opportunity to view situations with clarity and a new perspective versus being stuck in old patterns.[4]

Mindful Stress Response

- Respond by acknowledging the stress has occurred.
- Respond by paying attention to breath, thoughts, emotions, body, and instincts.
- Respond by letting go of expectations.
- Respond by accepting without judgment.
- Respond by choosing experience from stress to a state of balance.

© MaxFX/Shutterstock.com

From Reacting to Responding...

Take a moment and reflect on the following story outlining how your body might react to stress. You woke up this morning in a good mood. Today was your birthday and you were nearly finished with an important project, which you planned to complete before you left work. One might say that your sympathetic and parasympathetic systems were doing a fine job finding balance, as you had a good deal of energy yet felt relaxed. When you arrived at work you found out that you were fired. Your body immediately fired up the fight-or-flight response. The sympathetic nervous system communicated to the body's systems to activate only what was necessary for survival at that moment. The command was to release hormones that speed up the heart rate and elevate blood pressure, dilate the arteries and pupils, increase ventilation, slow down the digestive system, and release glucose from the liver. The soldiers in your adrenals sent the hormone chemical messengers, which rapidly began to travel throughout your bloodstream. You were now prepared for survival against a threat to the organic body.

The only problem is that the loss of your job isn't truly a threat against your organic body. It's upsetting, yes, but not deadly. Unfortunately, unless you learn to control this reaction and respond rather than react, your body will stay in this heightened state of alert and you can develop serious physical problems. Chronic oversecretion of stress hormones not only affects the immune and digestive system, but also adversely affects brain function, especially memory. If the stress continues, the hormones continue to flood your brain and can prevent the brain from laying down new memory or from accessing existing memories.

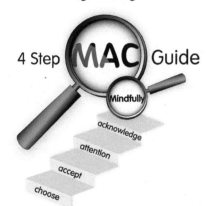

By dealing with the above situation mindfully, you 1) acknowledge your experience of losing your job; 2) pay attention to all of the thoughts, feelings, body aches, and any other awareness as a result of the situation; and 3) accept the fact that it happened and let go of any judgment you may have about yourself. Finally, you can choose to move forward and deal with the repercussions without getting stuck in the situation. You can shut down the fight-or-flight response, and activate your parasympathetic system, which will help you move forward to exploring new opportunities and heal from the event and celebrate your birthday. Mindful living can truly be a miraculous experience!

Mindful Living: Do You React or Respond to Stress?

List some the stressors that you are aware of in your life. Take a breath. Simply notice.

_____

_____

_____

_____

Describe your experience when you react to stress. Take a breath. Simply notice.

_____

_____

_____

_____

_____

DO NOT LEARN HOW TO REACT. LEARN HOW TO RESPOND.

Describe your experience when you respond to stress. Take a breath. Simply notice.

_____

_____

_____

_____

Social workers and other service professionals can better deal with trauma and vicarious trauma by practicing mindfulness and trauma release exercises. Benefits include relaxation, moving out of fight-or-flight, and burnout prevention.[5]

Let's reflect upon how you spend your time. Would you like to live a life where most of your time leads to happiness? Too often we are so focused on earning money, fulfilling the expectations of others and being laden with responsibilities that we overlook the fact that we can actually increase our overall happiness. Regardless of the type of work we do, most of us spend much of our waking hours in the workplace, even if our workplace is at home. Companies are realizing that a happy worker is more productive; therefore, instituting creative ways of offering quality time for employees pays off. Flexible hours, working from home, and cross training offer employees a variety of time options that employees can choose to fit their lifestyles. After all, we are all different and employers need to address how to generate the best performance from their workers. Choosing how one spends their time rather than mindlessly moving from one activity to another can provide increased satisfaction in time spent. We work to earn money but how we spend our money can impact our overall happiness. People often do not do a very good job of spending time and money in ways that maximize happiness. As various researchers have stated, "If money doesn't make you happy, then you probably aren't spending it right."[6] Studies have shown that people who spend their time with family and friends experience greater moment-to-moment happiness compared to work or commuting.[7] As you consider how you spend your time, think about whether how you are spending your time is bringing you happiness.

This Magic Moment

- Call a friend you have been thinking about and share positive thoughts or feelings you have about him or her.
- Imagine that this is your last day on earth—what would you do? Do that today.
- Take off your shoes, wiggle, and stretch your toes.
- Warmly hug someone you care about.
- Watch your favorite comedy and laugh out loud.
- Go to your favorite bookstore and browse through a new section.
- Cook yourself a delicious meal and eat it very slowly.
- Kiss yourself kindly.
- Take a long shower or bath.
- Sit in silence for an hour.
- Count your breaths for a minute.
- Do some neck rolls at the next stoplight.
- Watch children at play and learn from them.
- Spend an entire day thinking only positive thoughts.
- Walk into a bakery and smell all the scents.

Write down some of your magic moments:

_____

_____

_____

_____

A study measuring brain electrical activity before and immediately after an eight-week mindfulness meditation program showed significant increases in left-sided anterior activation and patterns associated with positivity in those who meditated versus those who did not meditate. In addition, the researchers found significant increases in antibody titer to influenza vaccine in subjects in the meditation groups compared with those in the control group. This study on mindfulness-based stress reduction shows the positive effects on brain and immune function.[8]

Think about how you spend your time. Remember that every minute used is lost forever. When you acknowledge this, you soon become aware of the importance of how you spend your personal time. Are you satisfied with how you use your time? When you completed your personal time assessment you may have realized that approximately one third of your day is spent sleeping. To help you decide how you mindfully spend your time, place the percentage of time you would like to spend in the areas that are important to you—for example, exercise, work, play, and sleep, relaxation, spiritual practice, relationships, and any other activity that deserves your attention.

My Personal Time Assessment Today		
Hours in a day		24
Minus hours sleeping		
	Remainder	_____
Minus hours working/attending school		
	Remainder	_____
Minus hours with family and personal responsibilities		
	Remainder	_____
Minus personal routine cares, i.e., showering, brushing teeth, eating		
	Remainder	_____
Minus voicemail, mail/email, phone, text		
	Remainder	_____
Minus other		
	Remainder	_____
Waking hours left for me.	Plus___Minus___hours	

My Personal Time Assessment Goal		
Hours in a day		24
Minus hours sleeping		
	Remainder	_____
Minus hours working/attending school		
	Remainder	_____
Minus hours with family and personal responsibilities		
	Remainder	_____
Minus personal routine cares, i.e., showering, brushing teeth, eating		
	Remainder	_____
Minus voicemail, mail/email, phone, text		
	Remainder	_____
Minus other		
	Remainder	_____
Waking hours left for me.	Plus___Minus___hours	

See if you can reframe your attitude toward "time drainers," those attitudes that keep you stuck in old patterns and take you away from what you want to be doing. Try to focus on "time enhancers," attitudes that open up opportunities that serve you. If you are organized and become more mindful of the mindless time spent on "time bank drainers" in your day, you may be amazed at how much extra time you can have for yourself. Take some time to reflect on your attitude, on what is draining your time, and how can you make the change to enhance the quality of your time.

Mindful Living

Because life is like the wind, changing all the time, we need to make adjustments in how we view situations so that our time is used efficiently. Instead of perceiving tasks or activities as "time drainers," we can reframe our beliefs and attitudes to experience them as "time enhancers."

Time Drainer Attitude

_____

_____

_____

_____

Time Enhancer Attitude

_____

_____

_____

_____

Time Drainer Attitude

_____

_____

_____

_____

Time Enhancer Attitude

_____

_____

_____

_____

Time Drainer Attitude

_____

_____

_____

_____

Time Enhancer Attitude

_____

_____

_____

_____

Time Drainer Attitude

_____

_____

_____

_____

Time Enhancer Attitude

_____

_____

_____

_____

In each point of the star *place the percent of time you would like to achieve* based on your personal time assessment results and your time drainer and enhancer activities. For example, add sleep, 30%, to one point, relaxation 20% to the next, and so on.

A research study of breast and prostate cancer outpatients showed that those who participated in mindfulness-based stress reduction reported enhanced quality of life and decreased stress symptoms.[9]

Money...The Road to Stress or Success?

Centuries ago people traded goods and services or utilized the one general store available in the community to supplement survival needs. The key word here is needs. Much time was spent participating in sustaining life in group interaction. Planting, hunting, cooking, child rearing, and housekeeping responsibility were shared. This group connection in daily living strengthened relationships and was done for the well-being of the group rather than the individual. Today, in modern civilization, we survive by working for money. Since money is a commodity needed for most of our survival needs, pleasure, and desires, we place a strong emphasis on its importance. The advances in technology bombard and entice us through television and the Internet with a plethora of goods to purchase, often with the intention of alleviating fear and satisfying desires versus purchasing anything we actually may need to survive. It is no surprise that financial stress is one, if not, the greatest stressor. Our need to buy and overspend is daunting. Think about this:

"If things don't improve, we'll have to close 3 plants and lay off 50 employees – or ask you to live a little more simply."

- Three percent of all children in the world live in the United States, yet 40% of all toys sold globally are purchased in the United States.

- Research has found that possessions do not make us happier but can lead to more anxiety.

- The amount of "stuff" Americans have is staggering. Brian Scudamore, a college student, observed a guy picking up stuff in his truck that no one wanted. He bought a truck for $700 and began hauling junk from people's homes to pay his way through college. He is now the CEO of a multi-million dollar enterprise—1-800-GOT-JUNK!

- Two-thirds of those using self-storage units own a garage and half have an attic, while one third have a basement. Self-storage is a 24 billion dollar industry, more than two times as much as the NFL (national football league).

- Half of all expenditures by Americans are on non-necessities. [10]

College students today experience various kinds of stress with regard to earning a higher salary after completing college, yet college student debt and various financial situations are the leading causes of stress.[11]

Personal Monthly Financial Assessment Today					
Item	Monthly Earnings ( )	Money Spent	Money Owed	Feel Success	Feel Stress
Rent					
Food					
Education					
Entertainment					
Gifts					
Travel/Transportation					
Miscellaneous					
Other					
Total					

Describe steps you can take to improve your financial situation from Stress to Success in order of priority:

1. _____

_____

_____

2. _____

_____

_____

3. _____

_____

_____

4. _____

_____

_____

Financial stress restricts student participation in peer activities.[12]

Personal Monthly Financial Assessment Goal					
Item	Monthly Earnings ( )	Money Spent	Money Owed	Feel Success	Feel Stress
Rent					
Food					
Education					
Entertainment					
Gifts					
Travel/Transportation					
Miscellaneous					
Other					
Total					

Describe how your life will improve by making changes in your financial situation from Stress to Success in order of priority.

1. _____

_____

2. _____

_____

3. _____

_____

4. _____

_____

Unfortunately college students may hinder the joy and achievement of the college experience when they are faced with financial stress, which often become more paramount than academics. Research has found that financial stress negatively impacts academic performance.[13]

Addressing financial stress mindfully may require our assessment of needs and wants. Research has found that earning more money does not offer as much happiness as one may think. In fact, research has found that spending money on others versus spending money on oneself brings more happiness. A study examining the correlation between charitable giving and happiness found that out of 136 countries, 120 found a positive relationship between giving and happiness if they participated in prosocial spending. This was equally true in both rich and poor nations.[14] Although some folks may be millionaires and even billionaires, they do not feel the need to indulge in excessive spending to achieve happiness. Take Biz Stone, founder of Twitter for example. Biz' life since he became a billionaire has not changed much in how he spends his money. He still drives his dented old Volkswagen Golf, did not purchase a fancy home, and gives much of his money to charity. [15]

What is the point of this discussion? Yes, it is wonderful to earn a good living and have nice things, but to what limit and sacrifice? Keep in mind what is truly important—being connected to people in a positive way, enjoying all of our living moments and above all, keeping it simple while living in the moment. This is the secret to success and living with less stress!

Increasing self-efficacy in college students may improve student financial well being as those students are more likely to seek financial help, which can reduce financial stress.[16]

REFERENCES

1. Bonifas, R., & Napoli, M. (2014) Mindfully increasing quality of life: A promising curriculum for MSW students. *Social Work Education: The International Journal 33(4),* 469–48.

2. Rogers, A. (1996, July 22). Zen and the art of Olympic success. *Newsweek, 35.*

3. Rippe, J., & Southmayd, W. (1996). *The Sports Performance Factors.* New York: Perigee.

4. Napoli, M. (2011). React or respond: A guide to apply mindfulness for families and therapists. *Families in Society, 92,* 28–32.

5. Berceli, D., & Napoli, M. (2006). Mindfulness-based trauma prevention program for social work professionals. *Journal of Complementary Health Practice Review, 11,* 153–165.

6. Dunn, E. W. M., Gilbert, D. T. M., & Wilson, T. D. (2011). If money doesn't make you happy then you probably aren't spending it right. *Journal of Consumer Psychology, 21,* 115–125.

7. Kahneman, D., Kruger, A. B., Schkade, D. A., Schwartz, N., & Stone, A. A. (2004) A survey method for characterizing daily life experience: The day reconstruction method. *Science, 306 (5702),* 1776–1780.

8. Davidson, R. J., Kabat-Zinnn, J., Schumacher, J., Rosenkrnaz, M., Muller, D., Santorelli, S. F., Urbanowski, F., Harrington, A., Bonus, K., & Sheridan, J. F. (2003). Alterations in brain and immune function produced by mindfulness meditation. *Journal of Psychosomatic Medicine,* 65(4), 564–570.

9. Carlson, L. E., Speca, M., Patel, K. D. & Goodey, E. (2003). Mindfulness-based stress reduction in relation to quality of life, mood, symptoms of stress and immune parameters in breast and prostate cancer outpatients. *Psychosomatic Medicine,* 65(4), 571–581.

10. Sqanburn, J. (2015, March 23) The Joy of less: Americans have more possessions than any society in history. Can we finally take control of them? *Time Magazine,* 44–50.

11. Lim, H. N., Heckman, S. J., Letkiewicz, J. D. & Montalto, C. P. (2014). Financial stress self-efficacy, and financial help-seeking behavior of college students. *Journal of Financial Counseling and Planning 25(2),* 148–160.

12. Heckman, S., Lim, H. N., & Montalto, C. P. (2014). Factors related to financial stress among college students. *Journal of Financial Therapy 5,* 19–39.

13. So-Hyan, Joo, Bagwell Durband, D., & Grable, J. (2008). The academic impact of financial stress on college students. *Journal of College Student Retention 10 (3),* 287–305.

14. Aknin, L. B., Dunn, E. W., Sandstrom, G. M., & Norton, M. I. (2013). Does social connection turn good deeds into good feelings? On the value of putting the 'social' into prosocial spending. *International Journal of Happiness and Development 1 (2),* 155–171.

15. Heilpern, J. (2014, April). Out to lunch with Biz Stone. *Vanity Fair,* 94.

16. Lim, H. N., Heckman, S. J., Letkiewicz, J. D. & Montalto, C. P. (2014). Financial stress self-efficacy, and financial help-seeking behavior of college students. *Journal of Financial Counseling and Planning 25(2),* 148–160.

MINDFUL AWARENESS REFLECTION JOURNAL

Choose one mindful experience as you begin your reflection.

Empathically Acknowledge

Describe your experience.

_____

_____

_____

Intentional Attention

Describe what you noticed.

Breath
Body
Emotions
Thoughts
Senses

Accept Without Judgment

Describe judgment; acceptance.

_____

_____

_____

Willingly Choose

Intention/willingness; new perspective.

_____

_____

_____

Mindful Mac Meditation

Describe your meditation experiences. What did you learn from your meditation experience?

_____

_____

_____

Mindful Daily Journal

TODAY'S Insight

Tips for Wellbeing

- Have Hope
- Accept Yourself
- Exercise
- Practice Mindfulness
- Express Gratitude
- Master Your Environment
- Find Purpose
- Stay Connected
- Be an Optimist

Date: _____   Make Today Count!

PART TWO

Courtesy of Maria Napoli

DEVELOPING YOUR MINDFULNESS PRACTICE

When we empty our minds, we experience the fullness of the moment.

ARE YOU BREATHING?

Courtesy of Maria Napoli

I breathe in and smile.
I breathe out and smile.

Breath

We come into life taking our first breath. We can live for days without food and water but only a few minutes without our breath. When we are first born, we are more connected to our inner self and basic needs: breathing, eating, and sleeping. As we become more connected with the outside world, we are faced with more stimuli that use up our energy. The unfortunate result is that we often develop a pattern of shallow breathing instead of the deep belly breath that we enjoyed as babies. When we take in oxygen through our breath, we experience a profound effect on our physical, emotional, and mental states. Sheikh and Sheikh write in *Healing East and West*, "The rhythm of the breath is one of the most obvious physical indications of a person's emotional and mental state. When relaxed, the breathing reflects an emotional calm and indicates a state where the attention can be focused."[1]

Think about this for a moment. Before a test, you might notice your breath becoming shallow. If you are surprised or alarmed or experience a situation that causes anxiety, you might notice your breath picking up speed. In addition, physical changes like tension in the muscles, nausea, and sometimes pain such as headaches can occur when your breathing changes.

We breathe 24 hours a day, generally without giving a thought as to how significant breathing is to our entire body. It does not take a formal education to learn how to breathe, yet this very important reflexive function is crucial, giving us information related to our emotional, physical, and psychological wellbeing.

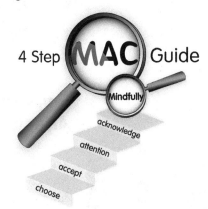

Your autonomic nervous system is responsible for your breathing, which is the reason we usually do not pay attention to how we breathe. We have discussed that the sympathetic nervous system signals the fight or flight response and the parasympathetic nervous system is activated for healing and rest. Research has found that slow rhythmic breathing stimulates the parasympathetic nervous system and decreases sympathetic nervous system activity.[2] Research has also found that both fast and slow breathing reduces blood pressure, although slower breathing had a stronger effect on the autonomic nervous system.[3]

Think for a moment about the regulation of your breath in different situations. Allow yourself to experience each emotion. Perhaps think of situations that elicit different emotions, and notice how your breath is stifled, restricted, smooth, regulated, shallow, or even unnoticeable. Are you activating the sympathetic or parasympathetic nervous system? T. N. Hanh writes, "We are not working on our breath. We allow our breath to enjoy itself. This is mindfulness breathing."[4]

When I'm...	My breath is...
Excited	
Anxious	
Happy	
Calm	
Angry	

MAC Your Breath

Oxygen is one of the most essential nutrients needed by the human body. We cannot live for even a few minutes without it, yet daily living with pollution, stress, and fatigue contributes to shallow or rapid breathing, and restricts the amount of oxygen our bodies receive. The following activities offer an opportunity for you to bring mindful awareness to your breathing so that you can enjoy the full benefits of breathing.

Taking in the maximum amount of oxygen into your body affects the respiratory, circulatory, nervous, digestive, endocrine, and urinary systems as well as the skin. Basically, your breath is your life source. Too often is taken for granted. We breathe without giving it much attention. "The average respiration rate for a person at rest is about 16 breaths per minute. This means on average, we

breathe about 960 breaths an hour; 23,040 breaths a day; 8,409,600 a year. If a person lives to 80, then that means on average they will take 672,768,000 breaths in a lifetime!"[5] Let's take a closer look at how your quality of breathing affects each system of your body. Keep in mind ways you can individually attend to your breath more consciously as you read through this chapter.

Empathically Acknowledge How Breath Affects Your...

Respiratory system—Acknowledge if you feel fatigued or energetic; notice if your chest is closed or open when you breathe. Are you eliminating waste daily, or are you "backed up?" Acknowledge if you feel any restriction in your muscles.

Circulatory system—Acknowledge if you are experiencing congestion or poor circulation in your muscles. Acknowledge whether there is clarity in your thinking and eyesight.

Nervous system—Acknowledge if you feel relaxed or stressed.

Digestive system—Acknowledge if you have indigestion or an irritable bowel.

Immune system—Acknowledge if your immunity is weak or you are lethargic. Pay attention to the frequency of colds or flu.

Urinary system and skin—Acknowledge if you are eliminating fluids regularly and if there is swelling anywhere in the body. Notice your complexion: is it dull or does it have color?

Well-being—Acknowledge if you feel nurtured. Are you having fun?

Intentionally Pay Attention How Breath Affects Your...

Respiratory system—Pay attention to feelings of sadness or depression as well as emotions of joy and happiness. Notice how the breath comes in your body through the inhale and how easily it is released through the exhale. Bring awareness to how you move through your daily routine.

Are you feeling tired and dragging yourself through the day, or do you wake up energized and exhilarated?

Circulatory system—Pay attention to any tightness in your muscles and which specific areas of your body are experiencing comfort or discomfort. Notice behaviors of forgetfulness or disorganization. Are you seeing things clearly?

Nervous system—Pay attention to your body, thoughts, and emotions and notice the times you feel relaxed or stressed.

Digestive system—Pay attention to your eating patterns. Are you "wolfing down" your food instead of sitting down and chewing well to stimulate the digestive enzymes, thereby activating the digestive process? Are you eating live instead of boxed and canned foods? Pay attention to signs of indigestion or constipation.

Immune system—Pay attention to indications of how well your immune system is working. Notice any signs of your body feeling energized or weak or lethargic. Notice your thinking—is it sharp or dull?

Skin—Pay attention to any changes in your complexion. Do you see new wrinkles, or dull or pasty complexion? Are your cheeks rosy and full of life?

Well-being—Pay attention to the way you feel loved and satisfied. Notice if you feel connected to others or if you feel isolated.

Accept Without Judgment How Breath Affects Your…

Respiratory system—Accept without judgment all the emotions you are experiencing whether they are positive or negative. If you notice that you are feeling tired and dragging yourself through the day, accept that awareness without judging it. If you are aware of feeling energized and exhilarated, accept your feeling of well-being and notice what helped you get there.

Circulatory system—Accept without judgment your awareness of any tightness or discomfort you may be experiencing. Accept the quality of your thinking if you have been forgetful or disorganized and not seeing things clearly. Ignoring these experiences will gridlock you into a stuck pattern.

Nervous system—Accept without judgment if you are feeling relaxed or stressed. It is shocking how often we find ourselves on autopilot in situations that do not serve us, yet we deny and avoid doing anything about them.

Digestive system—Accept your awareness of your eating patterns without judgment. You may have developed a pattern of rushing your meals, having stressful conversations while eating, and swallowing your food without chewing well. For lack of time, you may be eating more fast foods than live foods as they take less preparation. All of the above will affect your digestion and restrict or slow down the digestive process from doing an effective job. Remember, one needs a minimum of daily elimination of toxins through the bowels for healthy living. Think about this for a moment: Where do the toxins go if not eliminated? That's right! They remain in your body waiting to be let go!

Immune system—Accept without judgment your awareness of how well your immune system is functioning. Remember that when the adrenals are pumping stress hormones into the body, you wear down the immune system. You may notice that your body is feeling weak or lethargic and your thinking may be clouded.

Skin—Accept without judgment any changes in your complexion, whether it is rosy cheeks, new wrinkles, or a dull or pasty complexion. Let go of expectations.

Well-being—Accept without judgment if you do not have balance in your life. This acceptance of your awareness is an opportunity for you to take action to find ways to relax.

Willing Choose for Optimal Health

Respiratory system—Choose to take in more breath to deal with all the emotions you are experiencing, whether they are positive or negative. If you notice that you are feeling tired and dragging yourself through the day, make a decision to do something about it.

Circulatory system—Choose to take in more breath to deal with any tightness or discomfort you may be experiencing.

Nervous system—Choose to take in more breath regardless if you are feeling relaxed or stressed. Bringing extra oxygen into the body will support building new and healthy cells.

Digestive system—Choose take in more breath. Find new ways of eating with awareness, quieting the mind, and chewing your food well.

Immune system—Take action and take in more breath. Find new ways of stimulating energy and enjoying life more fully.

Skin—Choose to take in more breath to bring more blood to your complexion.

Well-being—Choose to take in more breath and explore ways to bring balance in your life.

As you can see from the above discussion, mindfully acknowledging, paying attention to, accepting without judgment, and choosing to bring the maximum amount of oxygen into your body through the breath are life-changing actions. Remember we breathe 23,040 breaths a day. It's worth your attention! This is one the simplest tasks we can do on a moment-to-moment basis. Bringing mindful awareness to your breath is the route to emotional, physical, and cognitive well-being. Start now!

Three-Part Belly Breath

This breathing exercise focuses on the three parts of your lungs: 1) the tummy (the bottom part), 2) the ribs and middle chest, and the 3) upper chest and shoulders. It helps clear air out of the top of your lungs where stale air, which needs to be let out, often is stored. When you breathe into these chambers of your body, you will experience the most complete breath.

To fully understand how air comes in and goes out of your lungs, think about how water fills up a glass. It first goes into the bottom and fills up to the top. When it is emptied, it first empties from the top and then from the bottom. Imagine that your lungs are like the glass.

Notice how you feel now. Relaxed and energized.

Let's Begin

1. Get comfortable. Sit with your back straight and chest lifted. Alternatively you can lie down on your back.

2. Slowly take the breath in through your nose.

3. Notice how the breath moves from the lungs to your tummy, ribs, chest, and shoulders. Notice your belly filling up like a balloon.

4. Exhale by letting the breath ooze out of your lungs slowly like a balloon losing its air until empty.

Practice the three part breath with the attached CD. Then complete the Mindful Awareness Reflection journal highlighting your experience.

As you read this poem think about the various sounds of the ocean. Listen to them in your mind.

The Ocean...Tides of Life

© ArrowStudio/Shutterstock.com

The simplicity of its depth, the ocean shares all it has.
The music of its waves provide melodies
So soft it whispers, So loud, it beckons me.
Its moods are fluid, nurturing. and stern,
a home for sea life, prey and predators,
sharing the dark and light in harmony.
A vastness so wide and endless,
creating space for imagination, dreams and mystery.
Its relationship with the wind,
a dance velvety smooth
and coarsely rough.
An array of colors blissfully pleasing to the receptive eyes.
White caps amidst the green and blues,
reflecting off the sun and father sky,
as Mother Earth awaits its visit of tides.
It challenges all who encounter it.
Wild and thrashing, waves high and intimidating,
Its depth inciting the excitement of adventure.
This ocean is life,
reminding us of the essence of change,
Embracing the existence of love and fear.
Its endless soul,
Its ever constant fluidness.
Its passion for movement, the ocean,
Our teacher, lover, and demon.
Reaching the depths of the unknown
and the changing of the tides, the ocean.

—Maria Napoli

Bring the sounds of the ocean to your awareness.... Ocean Breath

When you practice the ocean breath, you will hear the sound of the ocean. Let's practice hearing the sound before we begin the practice. You might read the *Ocean...Tides of Life* poem while you experience the ocean breath, or simply let yourself revel in your own flow.

First take in a deep breath,

Then let it out slowly, whispering the sound *ahhhhhhhhhhhh* with your mouth open. Try it a few times.

Now take in the breath and make the same sound with your mouth closed. Do you hear the ocean?

© Leah-Anne Thompson/Shutterstock.com

Let's Begin the Ocean Breath!!

Get comfortable; sit with your back straight and chest lifted. Alternatively you can lie down on your back.

As you slowly take the breath in through your nose, let the breath out keeping your mouth closed making the *ahhhhhhhhhhhhh* sound. (Feel the back of your throat gently pushing your breath while making the ocean sound).

Try taking in longer breaths and longer exhalations as long as you're comfortable.

Listen to your personal ocean, imagine your own boat, and let the waves sweep you away.

Practice the ocean breath with the attached CD. Then complete the Mindful Awareness Reflection journal highlighting your experience.

Energy Breath

The energy breath is an excellent practice to begin the day or restore energy when you are tired or need to feel refreshed. It is a breathing practice to cleanse and purify.

Where Did the Energy Breath Get Its Name?

Bring attention to your spine. Visualize your spinal fluid. This fluid changes pressure according to the rhythms of normal respiration, and gets a big shift in pressure during the fast and forceful exhalation of the energy breath. All of your cells become alive like sparks of energy.

Practice by putting your hands on your belly. Then just as you take the breath in, quickly push the breath out through your nose with some force as if you were blowing your nose. Feel your belly contract in a pumping motion.

A key point to remember is that the inhalation comes without much notice and the exhalation is concentrated and forceful.

OK, Ready, Let's Begin!

1. Get comfortable. Sit with your back straight and chest lifted. Put your hands on your belly. Place some tissues nearby since this purifying breath will cleanse waste stored in your nose.

2. As you slowly and naturally take the breath in through your nose, let your belly fill with air like a balloon.

3. Quickly exhale with 5–10 short rapid breaths, contracting your belly (this is the important part).

4. Remember to let the air naturally come into your nose.

5. The exhale feels like blowing your nose with your mouth closed.

6. Notice the inhalation is spontaneous; the exhalation is focused and forceful.

7. Notice your own personal rhythm, slowly taking breath in and quickly and rapidly pumping it out by contracting the belly muscles. Pause slightly after each exhalation. And then begin again.

Once you feel comfortable with the conscious rapid exhalation, the gentle contracting and pumping of your belly, and passive inhalation…slowly pick up the pace with your own rhythm.

Feel the Energy!

Practice the energy breath with the attached CD. Then complete the Mindful Awareness Reflection journal highlighting your experience.

Mindful Living

Practice conscious breathing for the next hour and pay attention to your breath. Describe what you notice.

_____

_____

_____

Notice a time during the day when you are feeling anxious, stressed, or fearful. During that time, practice the ocean breath for two to five minutes. Describe what you notice.

_____

_____

_____

References

1. Sheikh, A. A., & Sheikh, K. S. (1996). *Healing East and West: Ancient wisdom and modern psychology*. New York: John Wiley and Sons.

2. Pal, S., Velkumary, S., & Madanmohan (2004). Effect of short-term practice of breathing exercises on autonomic functions in normal human volunteers, *Indian Journal of Medical Research, August 120 (2)*, 115–121.

3. Mourya, M., Sood Mahajan, A., Pal Singh, N. & Jain, A. K. (2009). Effect of slow-and fast-breathing exercises on autonomic functions in patients with essential hypertension. *The Journal of Alternative and Complementary Medicine 15 (7)*, 711–717.

4. Hanh, T. N. (2000). *The path of emancipation*. Berkeley, CA: Parallax Press.

5. Meade, W. (2010). Every breath you take. *Herald-Tribune*. Retrieved from http://www.heraldtribune.com/article/20100112/ARTICLE/1121008

MINDFUL AWARENESS REFLECTION JOURNAL

4 Step **MAC** Guide

Choose one mindful experience as you begin your reflection.

Empathically Acknowledge

Describe your experience.

_____

_____

_____

Intentional Attention

Describe what you noticed.

Breath
Body
Emotions
Thoughts
Senses

Accept Without Judgment

Describe judgment; acceptance.

_____

_____

_____

Willingly Choose

Intention/willingness; new perspective.

_____

_____

_____

Mindful Mac Meditation

Describe your meditation experiences. What did you learn from your meditation experience?

_____

_____

_____

Mindful Daily Journal

TODAY'S Insight WOW!

_____
_____
_____
_____
_____
_____
_____
_____
_____
_____
_____
_____
_____
_____
_____
_____
_____
_____
_____
_____
_____

Tips for Wellbeing

- Have Hope
- Accept Yourself
- Exercise
- Practice Mindfulness
- Express Gratitude
- Master Your Environment
- Find Purpose
- Stay Connected
- Be an Optimist

_____
_____
_____
_____
_____

Date: _____ Make Today Count!

MAC YOUR BODY

Courtesy of Maria Napoli

When you listen to your body, you will learn all you need to know.

Our bodies are incredible machines that work 24 hours a day, seven days a week. If you take the time to listen, your body is always sending messages to inform you of what's going on. This chapter offers you the opportunity to bring focus to your body. If you take notice, you may be surprised at the many nuances being communicated.

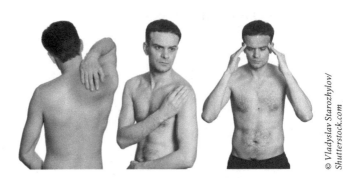

The body scan takes you through a brief journey of accessing information that each part of your body is waiting to communicate. The body scan is a true mind/body awareness where there is no judgment. One simply notices the opportunity to release tensions and stress the body may be holding onto.[1] The opportunity to prevent illness, manage emotions, and maintain over all well-being is a benefit of practicing a body scan. Take a few minutes every day and greet your body. Say "Hello my amazing body. How are you doing today? What can I do to make you feel your personal best?" To aid with this, the next chapter contains stretches that you can do on a regular basis.

You can manage stress more effectively when you pay attention to your body. Take a moment and reflect upon your body's communicators. Check the yes box to all that apply to you and add your own in the blank boxes.

4 Step MAC Guide

Mindfully
acknowledge
attention
accept
choose

BODY COMMUNICATORS	
Body	**If Yes, Describe**
☐ Neck/shoulder ache	
☐ Backache	
☐ Headache	
☐ Stomach ache	
☐ Joint aches	
☐ Loose bowels	
☐ Constipation	
☐ Heart racing	
☐ Facial strain/tics	
☐ Lip biting	
☐ Lip licking	
☐ Insomnia	
☐ Foot tapping	
☐ Hand tapping	
☐ Knuckle cracking	
☐ Chest tightening	
☐ Light-headed	
☐ Mind racing	
☐ Tuning out	
☐ _____	
☐ _____	
☐ _____	

Empathically Acknowledge

As you move through the body scan, take a moment to acknowledge each part of your body with consciousness. When you are on your mat experiencing the stretches in the next chapter, acknowledge all messages your body is communicating: pain, pleasure, discomfort, tightness, fluidity, struggle, and rigidity. Simply acknowledge each experience and self-talk during your practice.

Intentional Attention

During the body scan and stretches, pay close attention to your breath. Is it short, rapid, long, and smooth, shallow or constricted? Notice your body temperature and how you respond to it. Notice if you are resistant to taking yourself to your edge, and be aware of what holds you back from taking risks. Take time to reflect on any emotions that arise such as frustration, elation, avoidance, and joy.

Nonjudgmental Acceptance

As you navigate through the body scan and stretches, allow yourself to be mindful of any judgments that arise. Judgments are not uncommon, yet make sure you acknowledge them, pay attention to your reaction, and let them go. Be a witness to your experience with nonjudgmental acceptance.

Willingly Choose

At the end of each mindful experience, give yourself permission to move from old patterns of behavior that do not serve you. Find new ways of showing up and experiencing your body with love and nurturing as you explore avenues of well-being.

Body Scan

The Body Scan is best practiced standing. If you are unable to stand, lie down or sit.

    Simply notice what is happening in your body right now.

1. Focus on your feet. Are you leaning on one foot, leaning backward or forward?
2. Focus on your ankles. What do you notice?
3. Focus on your calves and shins. What do you notice?
4. Focus on your knees. Are they locked or relaxed? If they are locked, soften them with a very slight bend.
5. Focus on your lower, middle, and upper back. What did you notice?
6. Focus on your thighs, hips, and belly. What do you notice?
7. Focus on your chest. When you take the breath in, does it come in easily or does it feel restricted?
8. Focus on your shoulders and arms. What do you notice?
9. Focus on your neck, throat, and head. What do you notice?
10. Focus on your facial muscles, cheeks, chin, forehead. What do you notice?[2]

Body Map

Before the Body Scan or any movement activity:

- Draw an X where you feel tight or uncomfortable.
- Draw an O where you feel comfortable and relaxed.

Before

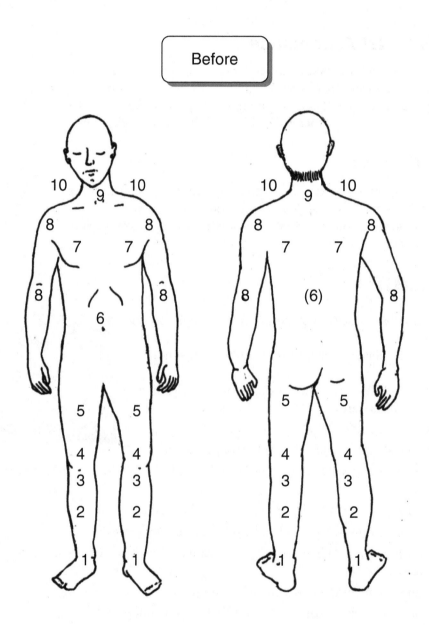

Breathe

© Zai Aragon/Shutterstock.com

Notice

© Aleshyn_Andrei/Shutterstock.com

Stay with it

© withGod/Shutterstock.com

Look Closer...

Notice if there is a difference in the way the lower half of your body feels compared to the upper half. Now notice if there is a difference in the way the left side of your body feels compared to the right.

- Take another Step—Take another Breath

Even Closer...

Deeply notice what's happening now in your body.

- Go to the place in your body that feels the most uncomfortable.
- Exaggerate that feeling by creating a stretch and moving your body to exaggerate and accentuate that feeling.
- Now go to that place that feels the most comfortable.
- Exaggerate that feeling by creating a stretch that exaggerates and accentuates that feeling.

The Body Speaks

If you gave a voice to the part of your body that felt the most comfortable and the part that felt the most uncomfortable, what would they say to each other? Let that dialogue resonate with you and be your guide to "what's happening now" in your body.

Go to your Personal Body Map and simply notice visually what's going on in your body now that you have completed the BODY SCAN.

Body Map

Before the Body Scan or any movement activity:

- Draw an X where you feel tight or uncomfortable.
- Draw an O where you feel comfortable and relaxed.

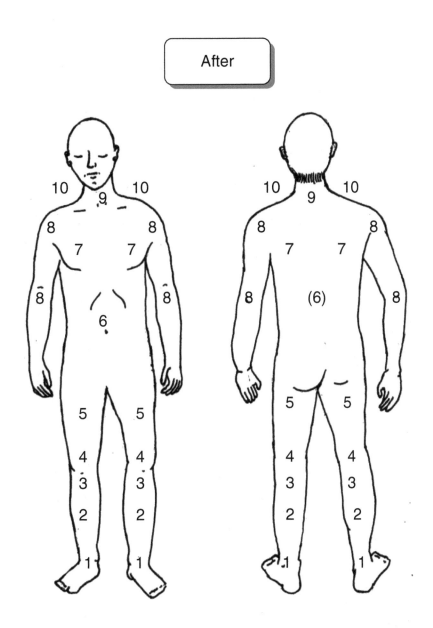

References

1. LaMeaux, E. C. About body scan meditation. *Giam Life.* http://life.gaiam.com/article/about-body-scan-meditation

2. Reynolds, N., & Lee, M. (1992). *Phoenix Rising yoga therapy training manual.* Housatonic, MA: Phoenix Rising.

MINDFUL AWARENESS REFLECTION JOURNAL

Choose one mindful experience as you begin your reflection.

Empathically Acknowledge

Describe your experience.

_____

_____

_____

Intentional Attention

Describe what you noticed.

Breath
Body
Emotions
Thoughts
Senses

Accept Without Judgment

Describe judgment; acceptance.

_____

_____

_____

Willingly Choose

Intention/willingness; new perspective.

_____

_____

_____

Mindful Mac Meditation

Describe your meditation experiences. What did you learn from your meditation experience?

_____

_____

_____

Mindful Daily Journal

TODAY'S
Insight
WOW!

_____
_____
_____
_____
_____
_____
_____
_____
_____
_____
_____
_____
_____
_____
_____
_____
_____
_____
_____
_____

Tips for Wellbeing

- Have Hope
- Accept Yourself
- Exercise
- Practice Mindfulness
- Express Gratitude
- Master Your Environment
- Find Purpose
- Stay Connected
- Be an Optimist

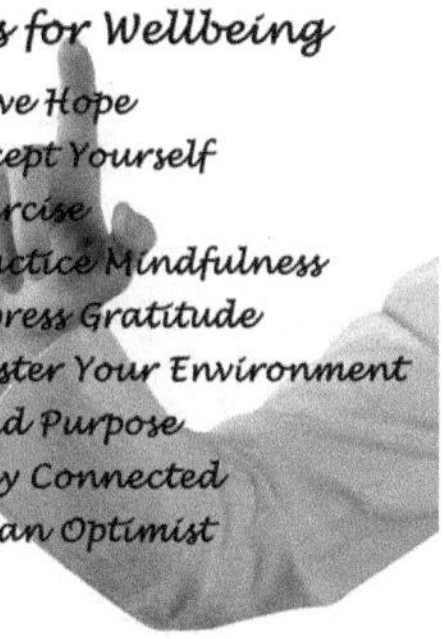

_____
_____
_____
_____

Date: _____ Make Today Count!

STRETCH YOUR BODY TO YOUR PERSONAL EDGE

Courtesy of Maria Napoli

This moment is the only one that matters.

Mindfully Experience Each Stretch

Our bodies are continually communicating with us, offering information about our emotions, instincts, thoughts, and level of energy. When we mindfully bring attention to our bodies, we listen to the information with acute awareness and thus are better able to respond and make choices.

Several studies over the last two decades have found that regular stretching improves performance [1, 2, 3, 4] and may prevent the risk of injury.[5] Some say that stretching reduces soreness following exercise. Research on stretching and muscle soreness have found that exercisers notice a decrease in soreness of less than 2mm on a 100-mm scale during the 72 hours following exercise.[6] Stretching before a workout is essential as it warms up the body; increases blood flow to tissues, which increases the removal of waste from the muscles; improves the velocity of nerve impulses to muscles, and delivers oxygen and food for energy.[7] The stretches on the following pages offer an experience of quieting the body and mind, providing renewed energy, and creating calm relaxation. The increase in energy stimulates better circulation, body strength, cell regeneration, and healing. Taking in the breath will lengthen the muscles, offer the maximum stretch, and take you to your "personal edge."

Remember to warm up before moving deeply into the stretches. You can choose your own warm-ups or use some of the easy stretches in this book to limber up. Think of your muscles as a sponge. When the sponge is dry, it feels brittle and hard; when water is added it becomes pliable and soft. When your muscles lack oxygen, they become tight and constricted. When you bring in oxygen through the breath they become limber and flexible. There are other benefits to increased oxygen as well. When you bring ample oxygen to your body during the stretch, the opportunities for awareness and release of stored emotions can occur. You may find yourself crying, laughing, or feeling sad or happy. Slow, consistent breathing as you move into each stretch will help elongate your muscles, enhance release of toxins and emotions, and bring a truly feel good experience!

Although there are many stretches to choose from, select two to four stretches and perfect them by doing them daily over a week or two. Repetition is beneficial as you will notice changes each time you practice the stretch. Move into the same stretch several times and notice the difference each time. Choose a variety of standing, sitting, and lying-down stretches, and work several areas of your body. Having a positive and open mind will bring you to your potential.

Begin your practice several hours after a meal. Allow your body to rest if you have had the flu, recent surgery, inflammation, internal or external injuries, or unstable blood pressure. Practice your breathing and relaxation during these times. Always consult your doctor if you have questions about beginning a new exercise program, particularly if you are pregnant.

As you continue with your practice, try some stretches that you are not attracted to and see what happens. It's important that you respect the limitations of your body, yet challenge yourself. For example, hold your edge a bit longer each time while focusing on your breath.

You may notice a surge of confidence and energy as well as deep relaxation after your practice. It is important to have a resting time following your practice. A good suggestion is to end your practice with the resting pose. This will give you time to reconnect body and mind. There is no perfect way to move into a stretch—only a correct way. We all have different bodies with our own capabilities and limitations. Remember, we are perfect in our imperfections. Honor them.

Enjoy your practice!

Seven-Point Guide

Mindfully Achieve Peak Performance in Each Stretch

1. Be a witness to your body.

2. Notice your breathing.

3. Pay attention to internal sensations.

4. Trust your instincts.

5. Embrace your feelings.

6. Hang out at your personal "edge" in the stretch, while moving into the fear, discomfort, and hesitation.

7. Enjoy the delicious sensations of release from the stretch.

	Witness
	Breathe
	Internal Sensations
	Instincts
	Feelings
	Edge
	Release

During Each Mindful Stretch

- Breathe slowly and deeply as you gently move into each stretch. Notice.
- Take yourself to your personal edge. Breathe, notice.
- Pay attention to what's happening in your body. Notice
- Breathe slowly and deeply as you more out of each stretch. Notice.

Mindful Practice Stretches

Standing Stretches

Palm Tree—Stand with your feet together, arms at your sides. Lift your right arm above your head. Rise up on your toes while stretching your left arm down.

Pine Tree—Stand up and balance your left leg; bend your right leg and place the right foot on the left thigh. Palms together, fingers pointing up, arms raised overhead. Now stand on the right leg and repeat. Remember that trees sway.

Peek-a-Boo—Stand feet apart. Bend forward, bringing head, shoulders, and arms behind your legs. Grab your heels with your hand, or bring arms behind you and clasp hands behind your back.

Squat—Stand with arms at sides, feet apart. Bend knees and slowly squat down, balancing on the balls of your feet. Use big toe for balance. With hands on waist or knees, look ahead and slowly come back up to standing.

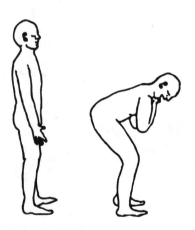

Seed to Tree—Come into a squatting position. Curl into a tight ball like a seed. Take a deep breath. Begin making tiny movements as you unfold from the seed into a full-grown tree.

Windmill—Standing with feet shoulder width apart, inhale and slowly lift your left arm overhead as your right hand slides down your right leg. As you exhale, allow your torso to stretch to the right and bend forward as both hands sweep across the ground in front of you. Repeat on other side, rotating the torso in a windmill-like motion.

  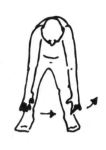

Standing or Sitting Positions

Eye Exercises—Sitting or standing, take a breath with head and shoulders relaxed and still. Gaze upward as high as possible. Hold eyes, and then gaze down as far as you can without moving your head. Repeat several times. Next, gaze to the right; bring eyes to extreme right corner of eye sockets and hold. Breathe deeply and relax. Next gaze to the left. Repeat several times. Next move eyes in a clockwise direction. Repeat several time. Move eyes counterclockwise, again repeating several times. Close eyes and relax. Rub hands together, feel body warmth, place hands over eyes.

Neck Stretches—Press head away from shoulders, gently tilting head backward so chin aims at ceiling. Then bring chin forward, pressing against the chest. Feel the back of the neck open and stretch. Bring head to center, tilting it to the left, lowering the ear toward the left shoulder. Turn head slightly to the side and slowly roll it back to center and then repeat on the right side. Feel the neck extend as you lean to each side. Remember to breathe throughout the stretch.

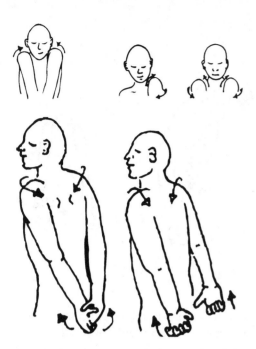

Shoulder Circles—Slowly roll the right shoulder clockwise, squeezing it toward the ear, then down, forward and up. Repeat several times. Reverse direction of circle and repeat on opposite side.

Finally, rotate both shoulders at the same time, then repeat in opposite direction.

Shoulder Squeeze—Fingers behind back, press hands away from shoulders, lengthening arms. Allow chest to open as shoulder blades squeeze together. Squeeze buttocks and gently tuck tail bone under.

Sitting Stretches

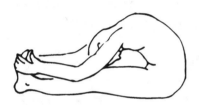

Toe Hug—Sit down, bring your legs together and stretch them straight out in front of you. Stretch your toes toward your head with both hands.

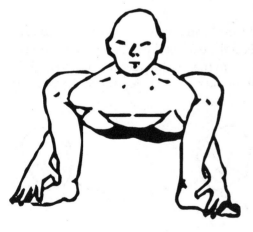

Grasshopper—Stand with legs shoulder distance apart and squat down, allowing your arms to rest on top of your knees. Bring your arms under, behind, and around your legs and touch your toes with your fingertips. Raise your eyes upward.

Bend and Flex—From a sitting position, stretch both legs in front of you. Hold your left toes with the left hand and grasp the right foot with the right hand and pull it to your ear while keeping the left leg straight. Switch legs.

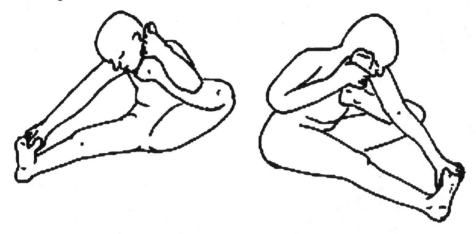

Cat—Kneeling on "all fours" like a cat, lower your head, and stretch your back up. Breath slowly through your mouth. On the exhale, raise your head and curve your back the opposite way. Look up and repeat several times.

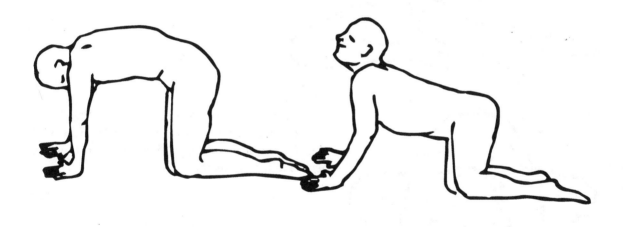

Twisting stretches wring out venous blood, which generally has low oxygen, pH, and nutrients. These stretches allow more oxygenated blood to flow into the body following the release of the twist. In addition, inverted stretches support moving the venous blood flow from the legs and pelvis back to the heart and ultimately through the lungs where it becomes becomes freshly oxygenated.[8]

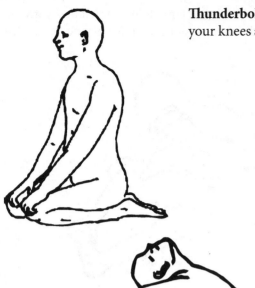

Thunderbolt—Gently kneel and sit on your heels. Put your hand on your knees and breathe deeply.

Swan—Sit on left heel, and slide your right leg straight back. Spread arms out to either side and bend back to your personal edge. Switch legs and repeat.

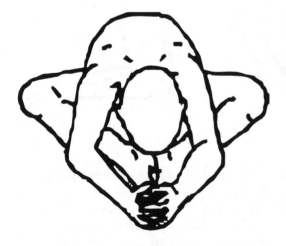

Kissing Toes—Sit on floor, soles of feet together in front of you, letting legs form a square. Hold feet with your hand and bend forward slowly head touching heels. Hold and breathe.

Bat—Sit on floor. Bring soles of feet together in front. Raise your knees and lean forward, slipping arms under inside of your knees, with palms down. Stretch your arms out to the sides until the back of your knee rests on your shoulders. Rest chin on floor behind heels or on feet. Hold and breathe. Slowly come up.

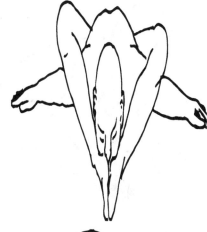

Royalty Pose—Sitting on the floor, bring the soles of your feet together and clasp your hands around your feet. Gently slide your heels toward your body and softly try to press your knees down to the floor. Keep your back erect. Hold and breathe.

The Open Heart—Bring soles of feet together, heels toward groin. Hold the feet. Press sacrum down, lifting top of head away from shoulders. Let knees bounce like the flutter of your heart.

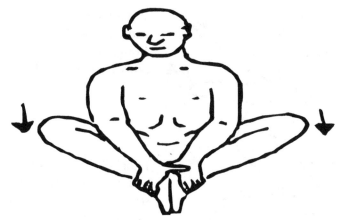

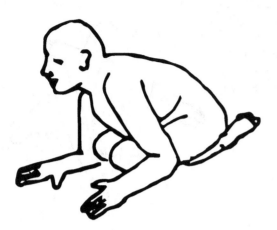

Lizard—Sit on heels, knees together. Lean forward and put forearms and palms on floor next to knees. Rest chest on knees, raise head and look up.

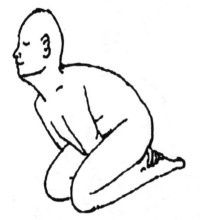

Pigeon—Sit on heels with knees slightly apart. Lean forward, lifting buttocks off heels. Reach back between your legs, and grab heels. Stretch head and neck up.

Wild Moose—Sit on heels with knees together. Sweep arms up and back, and raise your buttocks off your heels. Stretch arms straight back, bend wrists, with fingers up like antlers. Head up. Look straight ahead.

Lion—Sit on crossed heels, knees apart and hands covering knees with fingers stretched wide apart. Open your mouth as wide as it can open and extend tongue fully. Eyes wide, looking up, shout Roarrrrrrr!

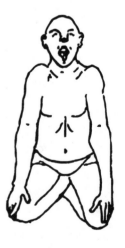

Bowing—Kneel on floor with feet slightly apart. Spread the knees apart. Stretch forward, palms together, arms, chin, chest, and buttocks to floor. Breathe.

Child—Sit on heels, arms at sides. Lean forward, forehead touching floor. Arms stretched back toward feet, resting along the legs with palms up. Make your body as small as it can be.

Puppy—Kneel on all fours, bring palms out about 12 inches away from body, lengthen arms, and keep knees still. Press chest down to floor while lifting tailbone upward. Hold for several breaths and let torso sway slowly from side-to side.

Hydrant—With knee lifted, rotate in small and then large circles. Reverse direction and repeat on opposite side.

Lying-Down Stretches

Bike Ride—Lie down on your back with your legs lifted off the floor. Rotate your legs in a circular motion as if you are riding a bicycle. Now add your hands. Have fun and add a bit of laughter too.

Knee Press—While on your back, bend your right knee toward your chest and wrap your arms around it as you bring to your forehead. Press for three seconds and repeat with alternate leg. Try pressing both knees at the same time.

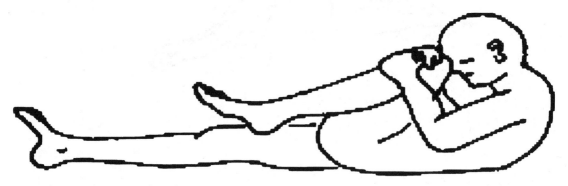

Half Locust—Lay on your belly, forehead on floor; arms at your sides with palms on the floor. Raise your right leg off the floor and slowly lower it. Do the same with the left leg while pressing down with the arms. Now try both legs at once—remember to press arms down.

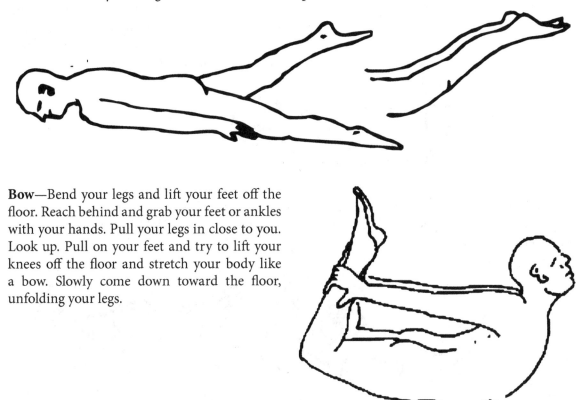

Bow—Bend your legs and lift your feet off the floor. Reach behind and grab your feet or ankles with your hands. Pull your legs in close to you. Look up. Pull on your feet and try to lift your knees off the floor and stretch your body like a bow. Slowly come down toward the floor, unfolding your legs.

Cobra—Palms and forearms on floor along side of chest; lower torso stays down; pelvis gently meets the floor; lift head and chest. Stretch neck up and back. Look up. Come down slowly a few times. Place palms on floor beside shoulders. Elongate neck and head and bring chest up like a cobra.

Alternate Leg Lifting—Lie on back, hug right knee toward chest with left leg extended on ground. Inhale. Slowly lift leg up, pressing heel away from hip. Lower leg and repeat several times. Do the same on the opposite leg.

Kissing Knees—Lie on back, feet together. Bend left knee toward chest, pulling it with hand clasped slightly below knee. Bring forehead to knee, keeping right leg straight. Hold. Repeat with right leg bent. Then do both legs together.

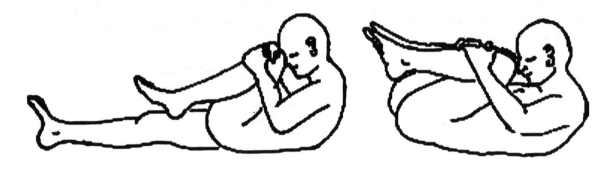

Womb—Lie on back. Hold feet with hands pulling them to your forehead. Raise head, touch toes to forehead if possible. Hold. Release and slowly lower legs.

Flutterbug—Lie on belly. With knees together on floor, bend lower legs toward your head. Place hands on back near waist, lift head and chest off floor and look up. Hold. Breathe. Slowly lower body to the floor.

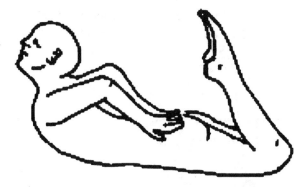

Seal Pose—Lie on belly, feet together and arms at sides. Raise head, shoulders, arms, and chest off the floor and look up. Hold for three seconds and then slowly lower body down. Try lifting your legs off the floor, look up, hold for three seconds, and slowly come back down.

Spinal Rock—Lie on back, knees in toward chest, slowly rock side-to-side. Relax neck, letting head be heavy. Repeat several times.

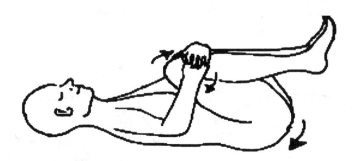

Sole Rock Press—Lie down, bending knees. Hold feet and press soles together, allowing knees to fall wide open as you rock gently from side-to-side.

Scissors—Lie on back, legs extended upward with arms along torso, palms down. Inhale, press heels away from hips, with legs spread apart. Bring legs together, crossing right leg in front of the left. Reverse the crossing of the legs as you repeat. Keep lower back on the ground at all times.

Head Roll—Keep knees bent, feet flat on floor, arms at sides. Slowly move head, rolling to one side, bringing the ear to the ground. Move eyes in the direction of head. Relax head and neck completely and repeat on opposite side, moving side-to-side.

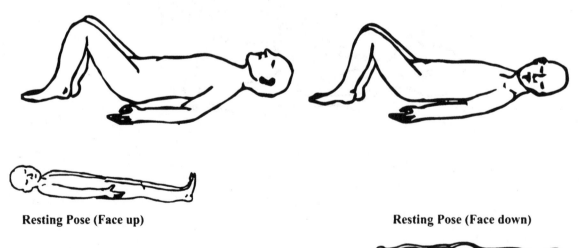

Resting Pose (Face up)

Resting Pose (Face down)

Energy Breaths

To fully experience the stretch, start each energy exercise slowly, deepen breath, let out any natural sounds, stay relaxed and loose, and then slowly pick up the pace. On the exhale, let the sound of **HA** become increasingly strong. The **HA** sound is a forceful exhaling release. Allow yourself to let the sound go free as it happens. These stretches are energizing and invigorating!

Bun walk—Extend legs forward. Lift arms in front at shoulder height, making fists. Exhale **HA** while sliding right leg forward, press heel away from hip while extending right arm forward. Repeat on left side as body moves forward, walking on buttocks. Reverse, walking backward.

There are many benefits when one practices yoga as it interrupts the stress response (fight or flight), facilitating a balance between the mind and body.[9]

Monkey Hara

Monkey—Stand with feet slightly wider than shoulder width apart, bend knees a bit and relax arms at side. Press soles of feet into the ground, squeeze the buttocks, and exhale **HA** while making fist with left hand and sliding it into the left armpit as your right hand slides down the right leg. Allow torso to bend to the right and leaning into the right leg for support. Inhale return to center and repeat on other side several times going side-to-side.

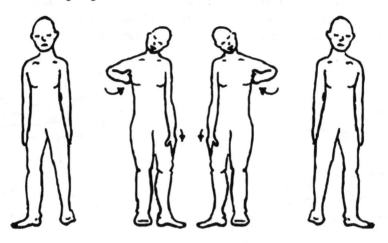

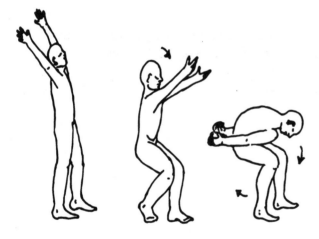

Brushing Floor—Stand with feet comfortably apart, swinging arms forward and back. Keep knees slightly bent, press feet into ground, exhale **HA** as you bend forward. Brush floor with finger tips. Inhale, return to standing as you swing arms up over head and repeat. Lightly bounce the knees and ankles as your arms swing down and again as the arms swing up.

Swing Twist—Keep feet shoulder width apart, arms relaxed by your side. Begin to turn your hips to the right, then the left, allowing arms to swing to side-to-side like empty coat sleeves. Exhale **HA** to each side, allowing head and eyes to turn, following the hands.

Airplane Swing—With feet wider than shoulder width, lift tail bone, hinge forward, and bring right hand to left foot or ankle. Extend left arm up and turn head to gaze at left hand, giving spine a gentle twist. Slowly repeat on the opposite side. While inhaling, return to center and then exhale **HA** as you swing your arms to the left, turning head to follow your hands.

Remember...During Each Mindful Stretch

- Breathe slowly and deeply as you gently move into each stretch. Notice.
- Take yourself to your personal edge. Breathe, notice.
- Pay attention to what's happening in your body. Notice
- Breathe slowly and deeply as you more out of each stretch. Notice.

References

1. Handel, M., Horstmann, T., Dickhuth, H. H., & Gulch, R. W. (1997). Effects of contract-relax stretching training on muscle performance in athletes. *European Journal of Applied Physiological Occupational Physiology 76*, 400–408.

2. Kerrigan, D. C., Xenopoulos-Oddsson, A., Sullivan, M. J., & Riley, P. O. (2003). Effect of hip flexor-stretching program on gait in the elderly. *Archives in Physical Medical Rehabilitation 84*: 1–6.

3. Wilson, G. J., Elliott, B. C., & Wood, G. A. (1992). Stretch shorten cycle performance enhancement through flexibility training. *Medicine & Science in Sports & Exercise 24*, 116–123.

4. Hunter, J. P., & Marshall, R. N. (2002). Effects of power and flexibility training on vertical jump technique. *Medicine & Science in Sports Exercise 34*, 478–486.

5. Shellock, F. G., & Prentice, W. E. (1985). Warming-up and stretching for improved physical performance and prevention of sports-related injuries. *Sports Medicine 2,* 267–278.

6. Andersen, J. C. (2005). Stretching before and after exercise: Effect on muscle soreness and injury risk. *Journal of Athletic Training 40 (3),* 218–220.

7. Thacker, S. B., Gihchrist, J., Stroup, D. F., & Kimsey, Jr., C. D. (2004). The impact of stretching on sports injury risk: A systematic review of the literature. *Medicine & Science in Sports & Exercise, 36 (3),* 371–368.

8. Woodyard, C. (2011). Exploring the therapeutic effects of yoga and its ability to increase quality of life. *International Journal of Yoga July–December. 4 (2),* 49–54.

9. Bhattacharjee, A. S. (2008). Modulation of immune response in stress by yoga. *International Journal of Yoga,* 45–55.

MINDFUL AWARENESS REFLECTION JOURNAL

Choose one mindful experience as you begin your reflection.

Empathically Acknowledge

Describe your experience.

_____

_____

_____

Intentional Attention

Describe what you noticed.

Breath
Body
Emotions
Thoughts
Senses

Accept Without Judgment

Describe judgment; acceptance.

_____

_____

_____

Willingly Choose

Intention/willingness; new perspective.

_____

_____

_____

Mindful Mac Meditation

Describe your meditation experiences. What did you learn from your meditation experience?

_____

_____

_____

Mindful Daily Journal

TODAY'S insight WOW!

_____
_____
_____

_____

_____

_____

_____

_____

_____

_____

_____

_____

_____

_____

_____

_____

_____

_____

_____

_____

Tips for Wellbeing

- Have Hope
- Accept Yourself
- Exercise
- Practice Mindfulness
- Express Gratitude
- Master Your Environment
- Find Purpose
- Stay Connected
- Be an Optimist

_____

_____

_____

_____

_____

Date: _____   Make Today Count!

YOUR SENSES ARE CALLING

Courtesy of Maria Napoli

I feel the wind brush gently across my face.
I taste the rain so moist on my lips.
I smell the flowers pungent and sweet.
I hear the birds singing melodically.
How wonderful life is!

MAC *Your Senses*

Traditionally we have been taught that we have five senses, and some scientists even think that we have many more, yet we are often not consciously engaged in experiencing them. Hearing, sight, taste, touch, and smell are the windows to providing information to the brain from the outside world, whereas pain, balance, thirst, and hunger are the windows for the brain to respond to what is going on internally. Our five traditional senses are located in the cerebral cortex of the brain and each sense stimulates a different part of that area. Some of us use one or two senses more frequently than we do the others. Even then, we often do not pay attention to the variety of information being communicated through those senses.

Our senses protect us from danger. For example, if you hear a police siren, the sound will alert you. In today's world, we use our sight most often, particularly since the invention of television, social media, and computers. Our other senses were more finely tuned decades ago when humans lived in the open air, and protection and awareness from the elements of nature and predators were essential to survival. The ability to hear and feel the wind and to see and smell animal trails was not uncommon. Today, we are disconnected. We buy our clothes and food from a store, allowing us less time for touching and smelling. We probably would experience increased sensory stimulation if we were more involved in the making of our clothes and gathering of our food. In addition, we are surrounded by social media that continually bombards our cognitive awareness as well as concrete that limits our ability to walk on and feel the earth and grass, hear the ocean, or smell the wind.

Our senses are vital communicators that enhance and give deeper meaning to our lives. From gazing at a kaleidoscope sky to touching the soft skin of a baby, our senses are awakened and our connection to life deepened. Animals developed their senses for the same reasons. Vision, hearing, and smell evolved to help animals solve survival problems, such as knowing where to hide in time of danger.

Animals have different sense acuity than humans. Those of us who have animals often notice how they know before us that something is going on. Sometimes we are amazed at their accurateness! We may also notice their intense focus on smell. Although we have known that animals sense things more acutely than humans do, we did not know exactly how keen these senses are until recently. For example, one study found that dogs were able to detect chemicals from urine in patients diagnosed with prostate cancer.[1] Another study found that dogs were able to identify patients diagnosed with lung cancer simply by smelling their breath.[2] Other research has found that dogs are able to know when their owners decide to return home even though they are miles away.[3]

Needless to say, service dogs and other animals are able to save the lives of those afflicted with blindness, diabetes, cardiac conditions, post-traumatic stress disorders and various other medical issues due to their acute use of their senses. Animals are truly man's best friends!

Incredible Instinct: A Felt Sense

Along with the traditional senses, we also can identify what is sometimes called our *sixth sense*. (It is also known as intuition. All animals, including humans, are born with instinctual behavior.) First responders such as police, fireman, and physicians frequently pay attention to intuition in spite of the learned knowledge of their professional skills. (Learned knowledge is what gives people solid intuition. It is experiences and expertise that fuel intuition so this might seem contradictory.) Nurses use intuition daily and often move through their days seamlessly, perhaps not even noticing how often they depend upon this "felt sense" when treating patients. When teaching nursing in intuition, it has been said that information involves training of the senses, development of the neural synapses and expanding memory so that the nurse can make assessments.[4]

The particular nuances of each situation offer information that may be learned from experience and the body makes that information available quickly. The key is mindfully acknowledging those cues. Research has found that humans respond to situations before they occur. This may come as no surprise since most of us have at one time or another may have said, "I just felt it coming. I knew before it happened." Listening to our "gut" occurs often and greatly benefits us when we pay attention to its messages. In the past, we have not been able to explain these experiences but now we have proof not only that our instinctual perception exists, but also what happens during this process.

Our bodies are mean machines and work fearlessly to create harmony. There is ongoing communication between the heart and brain, stomach and brain, and messages are communicated through neuro-pathways all the time. A study found that our heart appears to receive and respond to intuitive information. There is greater heart deceleration *five seconds* before the presentation of an emotional stimulus when compared to a calm stimulus. The way the heart decodes this intuitive information is the same process as sensory input, indicating that the body's perceptual gear is constantly checking out the future. The same study also found that women were more attuned to pre-stimulus intuitive information than men were.[5] When we practice mindfulness, we are more aware of our senses and can more fully enjoy what they have to offer. Paying close attention to daily experiences will help fine tune your senses. Are you paying attention?

Your Nose Knows

It is interesting that some of us have a more finely tuned sense of smell than others. Have you been in a situation with other people and said, "Do you smell something?" and you are the only person aware of the smell? The opposite may be true as well when someone else smells something and you are not aware. There are many factors that impact our sense of smell that are not related to genetics or illness. For example, living in an environment that is loaded with volatile organic chemicals, eating foods that are full of preservatives, using chemicals for washing, makeup and cleaning also impact our sense of smell. We often do not think about how our environment impacts our overall sensory system and we miss out on the many scents we can enjoy when they are camouflaged by impurities.

Smell is an important sense for maintaining quality of life and unfortunately many of us experience a decrease in smell as we age. Research has found that African Americans and Hispanics experience more olfactory loss than Caucasians. What is the reason for this loss? Toxic environments and poor nutrition may account for this loss since known factors that typically affect olfaction such as mental and physical health were identical with white subjects who did not experience an olfactory decrease. Another interesting finding was that compared to men, women maintained olfactory function as they aged regardless of socioeconomic status and physical and mental health.[6] Did you know that 75% of what we recognize as taste comes from our sense of smell? Taste and smell use the same types of receptors. Imagine this: when you chew your food, you are forcing air through your nose, which carries the smell of the food. Unless taste and smell are working together, you cannot enjoy the various flavors your food has to offer.[7]

© Courtney Johnson/Shutterstock.com

As you age if you want to continue to smell the roses it may serve you well to breathe in clean air, eat organic foods, and use cleaning products without chemicals to prevent injection of toxic chemicals. After all is said and done, when you want to eat something yummy, if you cannot smell it you cannot taste it.

Smell—Did You Know That…?

- The part of the brain that processes smell is connected to our memory systems. Have you ever smelled something familiar and immediately recalled a past experience related to that scent? Can you think of one now?
- What makes us experience smell are tiny odor particles that can only be seen with a microscope. Millions of them are floating around waiting to be sniffed by your nose!
- Our nose can distinguish one trillion different odors.[8]

Analysis by researchers Jason Castro, Arvind Ramanathan, and Chakra Chennubhotla analyzed 144 different odors to see if they could identify consistent odor profiles. They found 10 dimensions of odors to be exact.[9] They are as follows:

Odors	Examples
Fragrant	Florals and perfumes
Fruity	Non-citrus fruits
Citrus	Lemon, lime, orange
Woody and resinous	Pine or fresh cut grass
Chemical	Ammonia, bleach
Sweet	Chocolate, vanilla, caramel
Minty and peppermint	Eucalyptus and camphor
Toasted and nutty	Popcorn, peanut butter, almonds
Pungent	Blue cheese, cigar smoke
Decayed	Rotting meat, sour milk

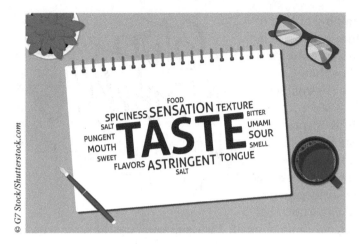

As we mentioned, taste and smell are intimately related. Think about when you have a stuffy nose. You may have said, "I cannot taste anything." Most of us love to eat, so to enhance that everyday experience we may want to consider fine-tuning our taste buds. On the other hand, taste is one of our senses that can serve us well or get us into big trouble by over-eating. Humans eat for many reasons and unfortunately we often eat for reasons other than hunger. Mindless eating can be caused from being stressed, depressed, or bored, or from unhealthy behaviors learned from childhood, temptation by clever advertising and the plethora of choices available to us. Sometimes family and friends pressure us to eat when we are not hungry. On the other hand, millions of people worldwide suffer from hunger because access to food is limited. The senses may play a significant role in savoring the little bit of food one eats when there is only enough to survive.

Animals do not have the same issues that humans have in choosing foods, as they are not subject to advertising, nor do they have the convenience of refrigeration and supermarkets. One might say that animals keep it simple as they focus on what they need to survive versus their desire, a characteristic that often steers humans down the path of obesity and poor health. Animals can sense through taste if their food is nutritions or contains toxins. The gustatory systems (taste) are able to discriminate between what is palatable and unpalatable. These gustatory sensory cells are able to recognize different tastes such as bitter versus sweet resulting from activating bitter versus sugar cells on the tongue.[10] For the most part, humans know if foods contain chemicals by reading labels, but unfortunately humans do not often read labels and frequently ignore them. Can animals be more intelligent than humans? Based on the research and the many health-related problems human have regarding poor eating habits, we can certainly learn from our four-legged friends.

"There is something wrong with the spinach.
It tastes good."

Taste—Did You Know That...?

- Taste buds detect sweet, sour, salty, and bitter. A single taste bud contains 50 to 100 taste cells that represent all five taste sensations.
- There are five primary taste sensations: salty, sour, sweet, bitter, umami. (Umami is the response to salts of glutamic acid.)
- You are born with about 10,000 taste buds, but this drops over time to about 5000 by the time we reach older adulthood.
- Taste is about 80% smell. Your sense of smell increases when you are hungry. If you pinch your nose, you cannot tell one jellybean from another because taste and smell are intricately linked.[11]

The Tender Touch

Touch is as important to good health as are food and water. In our modern technological world, we are less dependent upon our senses for survival, often resulting in tactile deprivation.

As long as six decades ago, theorists were writing volumes of books indicating the great importance of touch for healthy human development. Touch is our first language. Long before we can see an image, smell an odor, taste a flavor, or hear a sound, we experience others and ourselves through touch, our only reciprocal sense. We cannot touch another without being touched ourselves.[12] Early child theorists discussed at length the significance of touch on the healthy attachment of children.

The significance of touch for healthy childhood development is well known. Primary caretakers' attunement and appropriate response to their child's communication of needs during the first few years of life are essential to adequate neurological and emotional development.[13] Touch is often referred to as the "mother of all senses" as it is the first sense to develop in the embryo and all other senses—sight, sound, taste, and smell are derived from it. Montagu notes that the skin is the most important organ system of the body, because unlike other senses, a human being cannot survive without the physical and behavioral functions performed by the skin.[14]

Studies observing the contact between humans and their animals have shown that humans experience a decrease in fear and anxiety as a result of their relationship with their animal. We know that oxytocin, the touch hormone, is released from the endocrine system when we touch or hug one another. In addition, this hormone is activated during the human/animal interaction.[15]

Research has also found that touch creates a strong physical and emotional bond between infants and their caregivers, which continues throughout the child's development.[16]

In studies on passive movement of the limbs, preterm infants also gained significantly more weight, and their bone density also increased because of touch.[17]

The benefit of a tender touch is universal and has benefits beyond words. Some examples include putting your hand on a friend's shoulder when they are anxious, hugging a child when he or she is hurt, letting a person know you acknowledge their accomplishment, spontaneously pulling your partner close when they are afraid, Notice parents and children who are continually touching, or couples who maintain some physical contacts most of the time. Simple gestures such as taking a strand of hair and placing it behind a child's or partner's ear, stroking their face and sitting close together are all gestures of loving touch. Regardless of who you are or where you come from, as a human being you need loving touch. It is a universal commonality. Reach out and touch someone and see how it feels!

Touch—Did You Know That...?

- The most sensitive areas of our bodies are our hands, lips, face, neck, tongue, fingertips, and feet. There are about 100 touch receptors in each of your fingertips.
- We experience touch everywhere on our bodies. The amount of tactile sensitivity is related to the type and concentration of nerves in that part of our body. For example, our fingertips can sense the wing of a butterfly, but cannot distinguish if the weather is bitterly cold or unbearably hot.

The Happiness of Hearing

Perhaps one of the most important things to consider with regard to hearing is how we listen. Too often we rush around and even when we take the time to have a conversation with someone, we often do not hear them. We can fine-tune our hearing by developing the skill of active listening. Active listeners let the speaker know they understand what is being communicated without judgment[18] It may be a good idea to tune in your hearing when you are speaking and turn on your active listening skills! You might be surprised at how much more you learn and improve the connection between you and those with whom you connect both in relationship and casual interactions.

Hearing—Did You Know That...?

- Fish do not have ears, but they can hear pressure changes through ridges on their body.
- The ear continues to hear sounds, even while you sleep.
- Sound travels at the speed of 1,130 feet per second, or 770 miles per hour.
- Dogs can hear much higher frequencies than humans.
- Ears not only help you hear, but also aid in balance.
- Sitting in front of the speakers at a rock concert can expose you to 120 decibels, which will begin to damage hearing in only 7½ minutes.

Seeing Is Believing

Seeing is undoubtedly the sense we use the most. How often do we actually think about taking care of our eyes? Many nutrients like cod liver oil, leafy greens, broccoli, peas and avocado have lutein and zeaxanthin that support eye health. Eggs also contain vitamin A, which can protect against night blindness and dry eyes. Whole grains contain vitamin E, zinc, and niacin, which also improve overall eye health. Citrus fruits and berries contain vitamin C, which can reduce cataract risk. Nuts such as pistachios, walnuts and almonds and fish such as salmon, tuna, sardines and mackerel contain high omega 3 fatty acids that boost eye health. Kidney beans, black-eyed peas, and lentils contain bioflavonoids and zinc that protect the retina. Sunflower seeds contain vitamin E and zinc. If you eat beef—preferable grass fed—it contains zinc and helps your body absorb vitamin A. It can also reduce the risk of advanced age related macular degeneration.[19]

© paffy/Shutterstock.com

Have you ever thought about why we blink? Although blinking lubricates our eyeballs and protects them from blowing debris, research has found that the very brief moments we close our eyes assist us in organizing our thoughts and attention. It may seem that we blink randomly, but research has found that we blink at predictable times. For example, when reading we blink after each sentence. If you are in a group that is watching a video, everyone tends to blink at the same time. Some researchers postulate that we blink to have a mini resting point that shuts off visual stimuli, which allows us to focus our attention. When we blink, we may be taking a minute vacation of relaxation![20]

We process all information through our senses

the presuppositions of nlp

© CartoonStock.com

Sight—Did You Know That...?

- The eye muscle is the fastest reacting muscle of the whole body. It contracts in less than 1/100th of a second.
- Each time you blink, you shut your eyes for 0.3 second. This means your eyes are closed at least 30 minutes a day just from blinking.[21]
- Prolonged exposure to UV radiation damages the surface tissues of the eye as well as the retina and the lens. The best defense is to look for sunglasses that block all UV radiation up to 400 nanometers, which is equivalent to blocking 100 percent of UV rays.[22]

4 Step **MAC** Guide
Mindfully
acknowledge
attention
accept
choose

MAC Your Senses

As we discussed earlier, your senses are the windows to the outside world and the thermostat to your internal needs, such as hunger and thirst. Imagine how different your life would be if you tuned into all of your senses with every experience. Each situation would be intensified and experienced more fully.

Empathically Acknowledge

Instead of focusing on one sense at a time, broaden your observation. For example, when eating, notice the taste as well the smell, sounds, and vision of what you eat even before you take a bite. Acknowledge every situation you encounter with all of your senses.

Intentional Attention

Pay attention to emotions that arise, change in body temperature, texture of your skin, and thoughts as you acknowledge the various experience of each sense in each situation.

Nonjudgmental Acceptance

Allow yourself to take the time without judgment to simply become immersed in your sensory experience. Let go of your and others' judgment and negative talk, and give yourself an optimal opportunity to satisfy each sense with each situation.

Willingly Choose

If there is any holding back, judgment, avoidance, and negative self-talk in tuning into your senses, give yourself permission to move forward out of old patterns of limitation and into new avenues of sensory exhilaration!

Child Baking Cookies

You might relate to the following story. Todd lost his grandmother several years ago. He was very close to her and spent many of his younger years sitting in her kitchen helping her bake. The loss of her companionship and love was so great that he could not cry or mourn. One day he was passing a bakery and was drawn to a familiar smell. He followed his nose into the bakery and saw his favorite cookies that he spent years baking and eating with his grandmother. His mouth began to water and his body temperature rose. Memories of his experiences flooded his emotions and he began to cry. When he went home, he called his parents and for the first time was able to talk about his memories and feelings about his grandmother.

This is an example of how paying attention to our senses can offer information critical to our transformation as well as adding a deeper dimension to our everyday lives. Can you think of an experience where a sound, smell, taste, or vision brought new awareness?

© photobank.kiev.ua/Shutterstock.com

Elementary school teachers participated in mindfulness training program with their students where attention to breath, body, movement, and sensorimotor activities was employed. Results of interviews with the teachers revealed that the teachers used the mindfulness skills to: 1) aid in curriculum development and implementation; 2) deal with conflict and anxiety; 3) improve the quality of their personal lives in and out of the classroom; and 4) facilitate positive changes in the classroom.[23]

Sensory Explosion!

Taste, Smell, Touch, and See What You Are Eating

A century ago, providing a meal for the family required a full day's work. Hunting, farming, churning butter, fishing, and general food preparation involved the hands of many family members. In general, the average family ate three freshly-cooked meals a day. Most people worked physically and needed the relaxation time that came with sitting down with the family for a meal. Families gathered together to prepare meals, facilitating the familial connection and offering intimacy, communication, guidance, and support. One can imagine that eating was very much a mindful experience versus the hectic experience common in Western society. Sitting down for a meal is too often a notion of the past. In many ways fast food has replaced the human connection once enjoyed by sitting down for meals prepared and eaten together. The togetherness of eating with friends and family becomes closely related to love, comfort, and stress as well as supplying nutrients for the demands of metabolism and growth.[24] You might ask yourself what you can do to provide a meal for yourself and/or others that brings joy and nourishment.

© Helder Almeida/Shutterstock.com

Courtesy of Maria Napoli

Bringing awareness to your eating patterns can enhance the quality of your experience and offer information to make changes in habits that are not healthy. Take the story of Jeremy. He developed a mindless pattern of snacking on his favorite treats throughout the day and evening. He spent a great deal of energy berating himself for not having control over his "Nagging Nibbler." The more he berated himself, the more power his "Nagging Nibbler" acquired. Following the 4 Step MAC Guide, Jeremy acknowledged his desire for snacks, paid attention to feeling bored and to his negative self-talk, and accepted his experience without judgment. He made a list of more nutritious foods that he enjoyed and praised himself when eating healthy. Jeremy was able to make a choice toward changing his snacking pattern from "Nagging Nibbler" to "Nutritious Nurturer."

Mindful Eating

1. During one meal this week, eat slowly and chew your food well
   (25–50 chews stimulate digestive enzymes). Describe your experience.

   _____

   _____

   _____

   _____

   _____

2. Enjoy a meal this week with a positive attitude. It stimulates digestion
   and enjoyment while eating. Describe your experience.

   _____

   _____

   _____

   _____

   _____

3. Prepare fresh foods to receive the most nutrition from your meals.
   Notice the texture and smells of the food. Describe your experience.

   _____

   _____

   _____

   _____

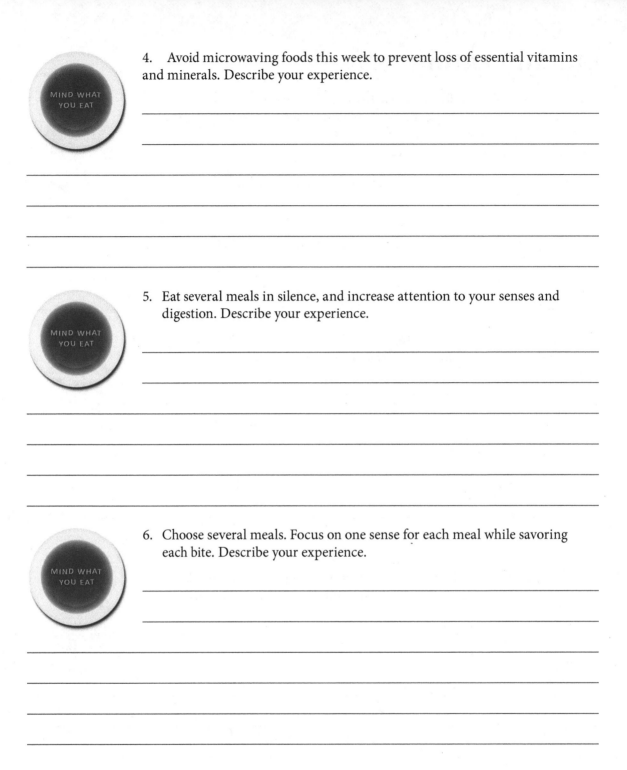

4. Avoid microwaving foods this week to prevent loss of essential vitamins and minerals. Describe your experience.

_____

_____

_____

_____

_____

5. Eat several meals in silence, and increase attention to your senses and digestion. Describe your experience.

_____

_____

_____

_____

_____

6. Choose several meals. Focus on one sense for each meal while savoring each bite. Describe your experience.

_____

_____

_____

_____

_____

Your Sensory Brain

"Everything we know about the world comes to us through our senses. Traditionally, we were thought to have just five of them—vision, hearing, touch, smell, and taste. Scientists now recognize that we have several additional kinds of sensations, such as pain, pressure, temperature, joint position, muscle sense, and movement, but these are generally included under "touch." Researchers know that nearly all sensory signals go first to a relay station in the thalamus, a central structure in the brain. The messages then travel to primary sensory areas in the cortex (a different area for each sense), where they are modified and sent on to "higher" regions of the brain. Somewhere along the way, the brain figures out what the messages mean.[25]

Mindfully Touch—Pressure Energy Detected by the Skin

- Touch the fabric gently the next time you get dressed.
- The next time you hug someone, hold the hug for two delicious minutes.
- Hug yourself often.
- Gently tickle your skin and enjoy the smile.

Describe your experience.

_____

_____

_____

_____

Mindfully Taste—Chemical Energy Detected by the Tongue

- Take small bites of your food and relish every morsel.
- Chew your next glass of juice and notice the taste.
- Savor your next dish of ice cream with slow licks.

Describe your experience.

_____

_____

_____

_____

Mindfully Smell—Chemical Energy and Shape of Molecules Detected by the Nose

- Stop and smell your breath, skin, and clothing.
- After putting on cologne or lotion, stop a minute and smell the fragrance.
- Sniff your next meal for a few extra minutes before eating.
- Wake up early and smell the morning air. Describe your experience. Breathe and simply notice.

Describe your experience. Breathe and simply notice.

_____

_____

_____

_____

Mindfully Hear—Sound Energy Detected by the Ears

- Feel the bristles of your toothbrush.
- Stop and listen to your breath.
- Leave yourself a voice message with loving words and listen to it for one week.
- Listen to a new piece of music.

Describe your experience. Breathe and simply notice.

_____

_____

_____

_____

Mindfully See—Light Energy Detected by the Eyes

- Look at yourself in the mirror for a long time.
- Sit in a room in your house that you don't ordinarily sit in and notice.
- Watch a sunset and then a sunrise.

Describe your experience. Breathe and simply notice.

_____

_____

_____

_____

Mindful Sixth Sense—Gut or Instinct

- Sit in silence and let your thoughts flow.
- Listen to your instincts.
- Enjoy the next déjà vu.

Describe your experience. Breathe and simply notice.

_____

_____

_____

_____

Mindful Temperature—Heat Energy Detected by the Skin but With Different Nerve Endings Than for Touch

- Enjoy your morning face wash.
- Notice how the air feels early in the day and then later at night.

Describe your experience. Breathe and simply notice.

_____

_____

_____

_____

Mindful Balance—Gravity Energy Detected by the Inner Ear

- Move gracefully in the pine tree stretch (see page 91). Watch yourself sway and then balance.
- Hop on one foot and then the other while laughing out loud.

Describe your experience. Breathe and simply notice.

_____

_____

_____

_____

Connecting with the Earth

Choose a few stretches from Chapter 6.

- Notice how your body feels.
- Hold the stretch as long as you can.
- Find a place where you can walk without your shoes (with your socks on or off).
- Feel your feet as you walk slowly on the grass or earth.
- Focus on your feet and simply notice what your feel.
- Notice what your sense of smell and taste are telling you.

Describe your experience. Breathe and simply notice.

_____

_____

_____

_____

- Pay attention to your breath.
- Enjoy a few stretches. Notice how your body feels. Hold the stretch; and let go.

Take a nature walk in silence. Close your eyes and listen very carefully to all the sounds above, near, far, close by.
Describe your experience; Breathe. What did you notice?

© Kostiantyn/Shutterstock.com

_____

_____

_____

_____

Alive With My Senses

- Begin with the ocean breath.
- Try some sitting stretches.
- Breathe and hold the stretch.
- Sit in a comfortable position.
- Pay attention to your ocean breath.

The Familiar Can Become a New Adventure

- Begin with the three-part breath.
- Try a few standing and sitting stretches.
- Breathe and hold the stretch.
- Think about your favorite place and the activity that you do every day in that place (a sport, personal care, being with a friend, parent, partner, etc.).
- Now imagine you are in that place, either alone or with someone, and use all your senses to notice what's going on around you.

Courtesy of Maria Napoli

- Can you experience the same thing that you see every day in a new way? Notice the little things, nuances, and the differences. Describe your experience. Breathe and simply notice.

Mindful Sensory Journey

Before you begin, put some dried fruit or pieces of fresh fruit and/or your favorite snacks in a basket or bowl, along with a beverage in a bottle with a secured top and a few small articles of clothing as well as a scarf or some sort of eye coverage. Find a comfortable place to sit, placing your basket of goodies within your reach.

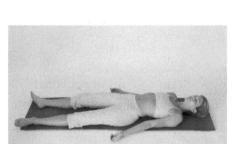

© Image Point Fr/Shutterstock.com

During Your Journey, Notice Each of Your Senses. Breathe Deeply.

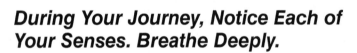

© Image Point Fr/Shutterstock.com

- Spend a minute or two noticing your breath. Pay attention to your personal body rhythm, listen to the sounds, and inhale the smells. Notice any communication your body is sharing.
- Place a blindfold over your eyes. Focus on your breath. Randomly choose something to eat from your basket. Notice the texture, smell the food, place it in your mouth. Begin to chew ever so slowly until the food is liquefied. Notice the process of the food moving from your mouth through your body.
- Take a sip of your drink and swirl it around in your mouth. Slowly swallow it and notice the taste.
- Take one article of clothing. Hold the article in your hands and notice the thoughts that arise when touching the fabric. Pay attention to your experience.
- Take off the blindfold and your shoes and socks. Focus on your breath. Draw your attention to your feet. Wiggle your toes, fan out your toes, point and flex your feet, make small circles with your feet, one at a time and then together. Do this several times. Notice any sensations that arise in your body, notice any sounds and smells. Notice your breath.

Find a comfortable place and lie down. Pay attention to your breath and scan each body part starting from the bottom and working your way up your body using this sequence. Here's a guide to read before you start.

Focus Your Attention on Your

feet…breathe…ankles…breathe…notice your calves…breathe…notice your knees…notice your thighs…breathe…notice your abdomen…breathe…notice your buttocks…notice your chest…breathe…notice your back…breathe…notice your hands…notice your arms…breathe…notice your shoulders…notice your throat…breathe…notice your facial muscles…notice your scalp and head…breathe…now rub your hands together until you feel heat…breathe…very gently place your hand on your face and rub lovingly…now place your hands on your heart…breathe.

Describe your experience. Your senses are an integral part of your life experience; pay close attention.

References

1. Taverna, G., Tidu, L., Grizzi, F., Torri, V., Mandressi, A., Sardella, P., La Torre, G., Cocciolone, G., Seveso, M., Giusti, G., Hurle, R., Santoro, A., & Graziotti, P. (2015). Olfactory system of highly trained dogs detects prostate cancer in urine samples. *Journal of Urology*, April 4, 1382–1387.

2. Ehmann, R., Boedeker, U., Sagert, F. J., Dippon, J., Friedel, G., & Walles, T. (2012) Canine scent detection in the diagnosis of lung cancer: Revising a puzzling phenomena. *European Respiratory Journal 39* (3), 669-676. doi: 10.1183/09031936.00051711

3. Sheldrake, R. (1999). *Dogs that know when their owners are coming home and other unexplained powers of animals.* New York: Three Rivers Press.

4. Green, C. (2012). Nursing intuition: A valid form of knowledge. *Nursing Philosophy 12*, 98–111.

5. Mcraty, R., Atkinson, M., & Bradley, R. T. (2004). Electrophysiological evidence of intuition: Part 1. The surprising role of the heart, *The Journal of Alternative and Complementary Medicine 10*, 133–143.

6. Pinto, J. M., Schumm, L. P., Wroblewski, K. E., Kern, D. W., & McClintock, M. K. (2013). Racial disparities in olfactory loss among older adults in the United States. *The Journals of Gerontology: Biological and Medical Sciences*, May, 1–7.

7. Koerth-Baker, M. (2008). The surprising impact of taste and smell. *Live Science* August 5th. http://www.livescience.com/2737-surprising-impact-taste-smell.html

8. Morrison, J. (2014) Human nose can detect 1 trillion odors. *Nature, International Weekly Journal of Science* http://www.nature.com/news/human-nose-can-detect-1-trillion-odours-1.14904

9. Dvorsky, G. (2013) The human nose can sense 10 basic smells. Biology. o9.gizmodo.com/the-human-nose-can-sense-10-basic-smells-1355489504

10. Scott, K. (2005). Taste recognition: Food for thought. *Neuron. 48* (3), 455–464. http://users.rcn.com/jkimball.ma.ultranet/BiologyPages/T/Taste.html

11. Binns, C. (2006). How We Smell, Live Science, May 22. http://www.livescience.com/10457-smell.html

12. Hunter, M., & Struve, J. (1998). *The ethical use of touch in psychotherapy.* Thousand Oaks, CA: Sage Publications.

13. Bowlby, J. (1952). *Maternal care and mental health: A report on behalf of the World Health Organization.* Geneva, Switzerland: World Health Organization.

14. Montagu, A. (1971). *Touching: The human significance of the skin.* New York: Columbia University Press.

15. Beetz, A., Uvnas-Moberg, K., Julius, H., & Kotrschal, K. (2012). Psychosocial and psycho-physiological effects of human-animal interactions: The possible role of oxytocin. *Frontiers in Psychology, 3 #234*, 1–15. doi: 10.3389/fpsyg.2012.00234

16. Underdown, A., Barlow, J., & Steward-Brown. L. (2010) Tactile stimulation in physically healthy infants: Results of a systematic review. *Journal of Reproductive and Infant Psychology, 28*, 11–29. doi: http://dx.doi.org/10.1080/02646830903247209

17. Filed, T., Diego, M., & Hernandez-Reif, M. (2010). Preterm infant massage therapy research: A review. *Infant Behavioral Development, 33*(2), 115–124.

18. Weger, H. (2010). Active listening in peer interviews: The influence of message paraphrasing on perceptions of listening skill. *The International Journal of Listening 24*, 34–49.

19. Ten Fun Facts about Hearing. American Academy of Audiology. http://www.turnittotheleft.org/educational/funFacts.pdf

20. Surtenich, A. (2015) Slideshow: 11 Foods to boost your eye health. Allaboutvision.com/nutrition/foods.htm. Reviewed by Heiting, G. October.

21. Stromberg, J. (2012). Why do we blink so frequently? Smithsonian.com http://www. innerbody.com/anatomy/muscular/head-neck/muscles-eye

22. Alderman, L. (2011, January 14). Let the sunshine in, but not the harmful rays. *The New York Times*, B6.

23. Napoli, M. (2004). Mindfulness training for teachers: A pilot program. *Complementary Health Practice Review, 8* (10).

24. Keeling, R. P. (2001). Food: Sustenance and symbol. *Journal of American College Health, 49*(4), 153–156.

25. Hughes, H. (1995). *Seeing, hearing, and smelling the world* (Tech. Rep. 20815–6789). Chevy Chase, MD: Howard Hughes Medical Institute.

MINDFUL AWARENESS REFLECTION JOURNAL

4 Step MAC Guide

Choose one mindful experience as you begin your reflection.

Empathically Acknowledge

Describe your experience.

_____

_____

_____

Intentional Attention

Describe what you noticed.

Breath	
Body	
Emotions	
Thoughts	
Senses	

Accept Without Judgment

Describe judgment; acceptance.

_____

_____

_____

Willingly Choose

Intention/willingness; new perspective.

_____

_____

_____

Mindful Mac Meditation

Describe your meditation experiences. What did you learn from your meditation experience?

_____

_____

_____

Mindful Daily Journal

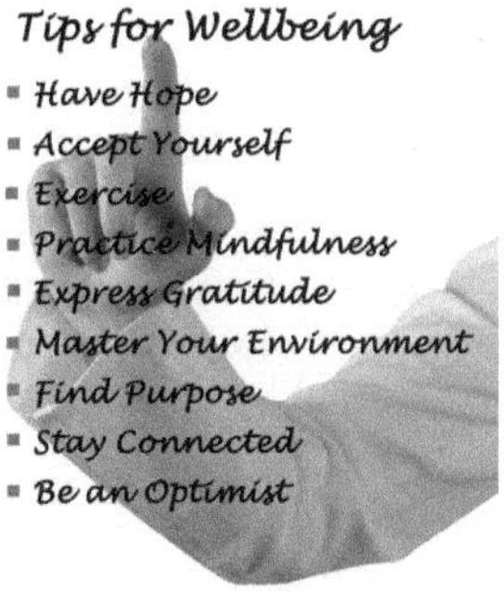

TODAY'S Insight NOW!

Tips for Wellbeing

- Have Hope
- Accept Yourself
- Exercise
- Practice Mindfulness
- Express Gratitude
- Master Your Environment
- Find Purpose
- Stay Connected
- Be an Optimist

Date: _____   Make Today Count!

CHAPTER 8

EMOTIONS RUN DEEP

Courtesy of Maria Napoli

Treat yourself to experience and embrace every emotion.

Emotions

So many experiences have been shared in our lifetime.
As children, the familiar, gentle hands, strong voices, and open hearts surround us.
As adults we go our separate ways,
Taking in the sprinkling of emotions displayed by those around us, savoring the bits and pieces, Enjoying the pleasant, a warm smile, a tender touch of the hand embracing your shoulder, and on those rare occasions, a magical kiss upon your lips so sweet.
These turns in life have shown too the depths of hate and judgment people inflict upon each other senselessly.
Many have been a victim of this wrath of unjust punishment.
Wherever you go, be assured that the love embedded in the vestibule of your heart has endless reserve to sooth your loneliness, wash away your tears and comfort you in times of despair.
The memories of those who have sprinkled your life with love, and nourished your soul have given you the capacity to love so splendidly,
With laughter, empathy, feather-like touches and your heart open and receptive to embrace the human spirit of love
Love never fails to rise to the occasion, oozing smoothly to embrace you.
The sparks of living are ever present, simply because you are loved and capable of loving.

—Courtesy of Maria Napoli

In your daily mindfulness practice, you will experience strong emotions that are sometimes pleasant and sometimes unpleasant. When we welcome all of our emotions with acceptance and curiosity, we offer ourselves the opportunity to fully experience even the smallest mundane event with a fresh look by seeing the details of the experience that may have been overlooked had we not been paying attention. After all, these are our life experiences, however small or large, and whether or not they feel good. Since we experience our emotions consistently, every day, why not mindfully accept and embrace them?

© Syda Productions/Shutterstock.com

Fatality of Fear

Fear and anger are the strongest emotions that prevent us from living mindfully. These stress emotions can have a fatal impact on our lives when they are not managed, if they become overwhelming, or even worse, if they are a part of our daily lives. When we move into the emotions of anger and fear, our nervous system goes into the flight, fight, or freeze response, telling the body that it is in immediate danger. When the human

© Ollyy/Shutterstock.com

© Ollyy/Shutterstock.com

organism perceives a threat, it activates the endocrine system, releasing an army of hormones to stimulate the body systems necessary for immediate survival, while suppressing those systems that are not needed for immediate survival such as the digestive and immune systems. This works beautifully when immediate survival is necessary but can be incredibly detrimental when we live in a heightened state of alert because our emotions are controlling us rather than we controlling our emotions. This is where mindfulness can be lifesaving; it allows you to step back and observe the emotions rather than become the emotions.

The negative impact of anger on overall emotional and physical health cannot be disputed. Volumes of literature have shown the often life-threatening consequences related to anger.[1] We often hear people say things like "I was so mad I thought I was going to have a heart attack." Simple phrases like this have become part of everyday language, yet the negative impact of anger on heart health is real. Research has found a direct correlation between cardiovascular disease and anger when the HPA axis and the sympathetic nervous system is activated, releasing stress hormones, which results in various events such as hemodynamic (blood to the heart) and metabolic (process of cells producing energy) modifications, vascular problems, and disorders of cardiac rhythm. This may sound quite scientific, yet the bottom line is that drowning ourselves in negative emotions can have a devastating impact on our lives.

What can we do about this?

Learn to respond versus react via applied mindfulness!

An interesting study with college students who viewed advertisements about creatine supplements (products that claim to enhance muscle mass and increase energy) found that students who used creatine and had no side effects exhibited less fear about the risks of using the products than those who did not use creatine supplements.[2]

The Frog and the Crocodile

A frog was happily jumping from one water lily to another when she spotted a crocodile swimming lazily nearby. She was a confident and playful frog, yet she felt her fear and stress rise as the crocodile came closer. The crocodile said, "I wish I could jump from water lily to water lily like you. I am so big all I can do is float around all day." The frog did not allow her fear to get the best of her and said, "You are quite majestic, Mr. Crocodile, and much too large to jump on a water lily. You would sink to the bottom of the river. Look at those rocks sitting so smooth in the sunshine down the river. I bet it would be fun for you to crawl from rock to rock while bathing in the sun." The crocodile smiled at the idea and swam away happily toward the rocks. The frog quickly jumped to safety and felt a sigh of relief. She said to herself, "If my fear of that crocodile got the best of me I may have never sat upon another water lily!"

Mindful Lesson: Fear can only control you if you give it power.

"I'm still not sure HOW it happened. One minute, we were bouncing ideas off each other, and the next thing I knew, we were using furniture instead."

Ails of Anger

It is not uncommon to find ourselves eating poorly as a result of negative emotions. Does this sound familiar? When we are angry with our boss or we have a fight with our partner, the desire to impulsively pack down a pizza or a pint of ice cream to soothe or cool down the anger occurs. Food and

emotions are highly correlated whether one does not eat or eats too much. Binge eating and vomiting were found to be associated with anger and increased with impulsivity.[3] Anger has also been associated with developing type 2 diabetes. A study of trait anger temperament in diabetic adults found that those with the highest levels of trait anger temperament scores had a 34% increased risk of developing diabetes when compared to those in the lowest levels of trait anger. It has been suggested that individuals experiencing high trait anger temperament may be more inclined to obesity, more likely to smoke, and to eat high calorie foods.[4]

Road Rage may soon become a new category of emotional illness! Driving is an every day occurrence for many of us. People take their emotions on the road, subjecting others to danger. Remember, "wherever you go there you are"—taking your baggage with you. We all may have experienced being angry while driving or have been the victim of another driver's anger and aggression on the road. It's not a pleasant experience and has had fatal outcomes for many drivers. Anger has been associated with a high risk of road accidents. Research has also found a correlation between angry drivers and crashes as these drivers lose control of their vehicles and concentration.[5] Fear and anger activate the stress response and hold us prisoner in fight or flight. It is true that we cannot live our lives without experiencing fear and anger, yet it is the inability to manage these emotions that keeps us cemented in the past and takes up space in the present. Due to the pain and discomfort that these emotions elicit, we frequently repress, deny, fight off, resist, or project them onto others. Unawareness or rejection of our emotions does not make them go away. Emotions that are repressed or rejected show up unexpectedly and control our experiences.

When we befriend our emotions and welcome them, we give them less power to influence and control us. Mindfully moving through the discomfort can put us back in charge of our lives. Let's take a look at the direction we all want to go—being happy! How does happiness and joy impact our lives? If you are interested in living a longer life get happy! You may have figured out at this point of reading through the chapters and practicing the activities in *Tools for Mindful Living* that ATTITUDE IS EVERYTHING! The plethora of literature written on the benefits of happiness and how being positive influences health and longevity is compelling.[6] A study of almost five thousand students who completed an optimism scale when they entered college were followed for 40 years. This study found that those students who were pessimistic had lower rates of longevity when compared to the optimistic students.[7]

The benefits of a positive relationship between animals and humans are well known. People who have pets experience joy, love, and companionship. Pets are part of our family, yet only in the past decade have we explored how many ways our pets positively impact our lives. We know how animals make humans feel, yet we may consider how we make our animals feel. Recently research has found that happy animals experience increased health, heal faster[8], and have improved immune systems.[9]

There are so many ways for us to be connected to life that brings us happiness. When one thinks of happiness, we must include the joy we receive from being in nature. Historically humans have had an intimate relationship with nature and a deep respect for it. We still need nature and nature still needs us, but humans have grossly neglected nature's needs as the growth of industrialization has moved us away from nature. Nature, like our bodies, always responds to healing and nourishment given the opportunity. Nothing has changed in this respect and we are now realizing how important our relationship to nature truly is. Research has found that there is a strong relationship between nature and being happy.[10] Most of us who revel in the beauty of nature do not need research to remind us of the joy we experience by feeling the wind, listening to the birds sing, hearing the waves crash in the ocean, being mesmerized by sunsets, smelling the flowers, and even feeling the dirt and grass under our feet.

The birth of social networks has expanded the connections among people worldwide. Facebook, Instagram, Twitter, blogging, and various other networks keep the conversations going 24 hours a day. It is not unusual to hear someone you know say, "I have 200 friends on Facebook." One wonders what that level of friendship really means? A survey that evaluated subjective well being compared face-to-face and on-line social networks. Having real-life friends regardless of income, demographics, and personality differences was positively correlated with subjective well being. Having real-life friends was more important for individuals who were single, divorced, separated or widowed than for those who were married or living with a partner. Interestingly, having on-line friends had zero or negative correlations with subjective well being.[11] Simply stated, it matters to actually spend physical time with our friends. We can hug, enjoy the physical space, share a meal, and pick up on nuances, all of which add up to feeling good.

© Randy Glasbergen.
www.glasbergen.com

"When you say you want to be 'just friends',
do you mean Facebook friends, MySpace friends,
Twitter friends, Buzznet friends, LinkedIn friends...?"

A study that evaluated happiness within social networks found that happy people tend to be connected to one another.[12] This connection speaks to the spread of positive emotions that can reach millions of individuals. Sharing happiness has benefits beyond the individual and can have a major impact on the societies we live in. If we spend more time considering if members of our community are happy and take into consideration the positive emotional benefits one can receive when

Rawpixel.com/Shutterstock, Inc.

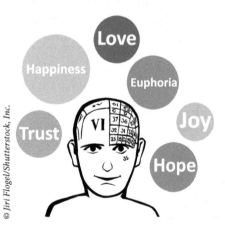

© Jiri Flogel/Shutterstock, Inc.

administering legislation, we could be living in a very different society. If happy people are healthier, it can reduce the costs of health care. When people are engaged in more positive relationships, there can be a reduction in crime, less abuse in relationships and overall, we can create an environment for people to enjoy living.

Living mindfully frees us from getting caught up in our emotions. The MAC steps are: *acknowledge* our emotions with empathy for ourselves, pay *attention* to how we are experiencing the emotions, and *accept* them without judgment. This is our ammunition to disengage from the hold those emotions have on us to assist in choosing how we show up for our experience.

When we mindfully accept our emotions, they have less control over us. How? By accepting our emotional experience, we complete the experience without leftovers or residue. We can move on more openly as the feelings no longer have the intensity of the original experience.

Let me suggest three ingredients to support your mindfulness practice.

1. Let go of past emotions. Holding onto emotions that have already occurred prevents you from fully paying attention to what is happening now and accepting it. In this way, you shortchange yourself by losing the quality of the present experience.

2. Experience synergy. The more you experience what your body, senses, and instincts are communicating, the more heightened your experience will be.

3. Do everything with love. It may seem like a cliché to say that love conquers all, yet I have not found a better guide to a happy life. When we live mindfully, we are better able to engage in our experiences with love, however simple, and strengthen our relationships, which are the "meat and potatoes" of living a harmonious life.

Children laugh between 300 and 400 times a day compared to adults who manage a meager maximum of 15 chuckles in 24 hours. Laughing lowers blood pressure, reduces stress hormones, and boosts the immune system by increasing infection-fighting cells.[13]

MAC Your Emotions

Emotions, like breath, are the barometer of what is going on in our lives. If you reflect upon your day, ask yourself, "How do I feel?" Chances are your emotions are changing from moment to moment based on the many experiences you encounter. These emotional experiences can be life enhancing or devastating depending upon how you accept, reject, or deal with your emotions. One might say that emotions are the spice of life, changing all the time, offering new and challenging experiences, and calling upon us to find new ways to express them.

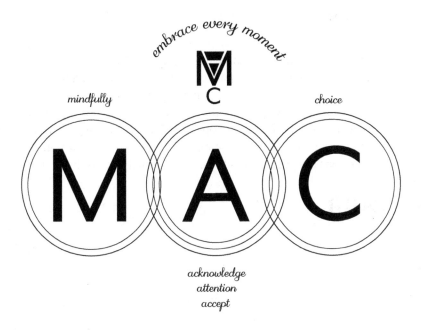

Empathically Acknowledge

Emotions can often be difficult to acknowledge. People spend a great deal of time avoiding, repressing, denying, and rationalizing their emotions. When we do not acknowledge emotions, we set ourselves up for repetition of the same experiences that cause us discomfort. Take a chance on yourself and acknowledge each and every emotion that colors your life.

Intentional Attention

We all have times when our mindlessness controls our emotions. When you allow your thoughts to take you out of the moment, your emotions are not fully experienced or experienced at all. Bring awareness to your breath, how your muscles feel, and to changes in body temperature. Most important, ask yourself how often you intentionally pay attention to your instincts.

Nonjudgmental Acceptance

Once you acknowledge your feelings and pay attention to what is going on in relation to them, give yourself permission to accept whatever you are feeling without judgment. Remember you are entitled to all of your feelings. The danger occurs when you react to your emotions instead of respond to them. Accept your feelings without judgment and open the door for intimacy and empathy toward yourself and others.

Willingly Choose

When we acknowledge, pay attention to, and accept our emotions without judgment, the window for change is infinite. Remember that what we do with our emotions has a direct impact on our health. The relationship between negative emotions and disease is not a mystery. This is not to say that we dismiss negative emotions; the point is that it is only when you respond to your emotions that you afford yourself the opportunity for change and choice. I cannot think of anyone who is happy being stuck in negative emotions, yet having those emotions is a part of life. It's what we do with them that makes the difference!

Mindful Living

© Keith Bell/Shutterstock.com

Emotional Awareness Practice

Make a list of the people in your life with whom you might share your emotions. Choose one person and share a feeling. Describe your experience.

_____

_____

_____

Notice in some small way this week a time you accept your emotions. Describe your experience.

_____

_____

_____

Make a list of personal obstacles that get in the way of dealing with your emotions. Take one of those obstacles and find one way to remove it. Describe your experience.

_____

_____

_____

Notice the flow of emotions for one week. Write down your experience in your Mindful Daily Journal.

_____

_____

_____

A study examining the effect of mindfulness on depression and anxiety on minority children found that those who received mindfulness intervention reported lower levels of depressive symptoms compared with those who received health education. Although both groups showed a decrease in anxiety symptoms over time, the mindfulness intervention group had greater decreases.[14]

References

1. Staicu, M.L., Cutov, M., & Davila, C. (2010). Anger and health risk behaviors. *Journal of Medicine and Life 3* (4) October–December, 372–375.

2. Kim, H. S., Sheffield, D. & Almutairi, T. (2014). Effects of fear appeals on communicating potential health risks of unregulated dietary supplements to college students. *American Journal of Health 6. Education 45 (5)*, 308–315.

3. Enge, S. G., Crosby, J. J., Wonderlich, S. A., Mitchell, J. E., Smyth, J., Miltengerger, R., & Steiger, H. Th. (2007). The relationship of momentary anger and impulsivity to bulimic behavior. *Behaviour Research and Therapy* 45 (3), 437–447.

4. Golden, S.H., Williams, J. E., Ford, D. E., Yeh, H. C., Sandord, D. P., Nieto, F. J., & Brancati, F. L. (2006). *Psychoneuroendocrinology,* April 31 (3), 325–332.

5. Sullman, M. J. M., Gras, E., Cunill, M., Planes, M., & Font-Mayolas, S. (2007). Driving anger in Spain, *Personality and Individual Differences* 42 (4), 701–713.

6. Diener, E., & Chan, M. Y. (2011). Happy people live longer: Subjective well-being contributes to health and longevity. *Applied Psychology: Health and Well-Being, 3,* 1–43.

7. Brummet, B. H., Helms, M. J., Dahlstrom, W. G., & Siegler, I. C. (2006) Prediction of all-cause mortality by the Minnesota multiphasic personality inventory optimism-pessimism scale scores: Study of a college sample during a 40-year follow-up period. *Mayo Clinic Proceedings, 81,* 1541–1544.

8. Erns, K., Tuchscer, M., Kanitz, E., Puppe, B., & Manteuffel, G. (2006). Effects of attention and rewarded activity on immune parameters and wound healing in pigs. *Physiological Behavior 30* (89): October: 448–456.

9. Detillion, C. E., Craft, T. K. S., Glasper, E. R., Prendergast, B. J., & Devries, A. C. (2004). Social facilitation of wound healing. *Psychoneuroendocrinology 29,* 1004–1011.

10. Capaldi, C. A., Dopko, R. L., & Zelenski, J. M. (2014). The relationship between nature connectedness and happiness: A meta-analysis. *Frontiers in Psychology September 5. Article 976,* 1–15. doi: 10.3389/fpsyg.2014.00976

11. Helliwell, J. F. & Haifang, H. (2013). Comparing the happiness effects of real and on-line friends. *Cedric Sueur, Institut Pluridisciplinaire.* Hubert Curien, France PLoS ONE 8 (9) e72754 doi:10.1371/journal.pone.0072754.

12. Fowler, J. H., & Christakis, N. A. (2008). Dynamic spread of happiness in a large social network: Longitudinal analysis over 20 years in the Framingham heart study. *British Medical Journal, 337* (a2338). doi:10.1136/bmj.a2338

13. Court, H. (2007, January 5). Laughter is the best medicine. *Gazette and Herald.*

14. Sing, L. N. N., Lancioni, G. E., Winton A. S. W., Sing, J., Curtis, W. J., Whaler, R. G., & McAleavey, K. M. (2007). Mindful parenting decreases aggression and increases social behavior in children with developmental disabilities. *Behavior Modification, 31*(6), 749–771.

MINDFUL AWARENESS REFLECTION JOURNAL

Choose one mindful experience as you begin your reflection.

Empathically Acknowledge

Describe your experience.

_____

_____

_____

Intentional Attention

Describe what you noticed.

Breath
Body
Emotions
Thoughts
Senses

Accept Without Judgment

Describe judgment; acceptance.

_____

_____

_____

Willingly Choose

Intention/willingness; new perspective.

_____

_____

_____

Mindful Mac Meditation

Describe your meditation experiences. What did you learn from your meditation experience?

_____

_____

_____

Mindful Daily Journal

TODAY'S Insight

_____

_____

_____

_____

_____

_____

_____

_____

_____

_____

_____

_____

_____

_____

_____

_____

_____

_____

_____

_____

_____

_____

_____

_____

_____

_____

_____

_____

_____

Tips for Wellbeing

- _Have Hope_
- _Accept Yourself_
- _Exercise_
- _Practice Mindfulness_
- _Express Gratitude_
- _Master Your Environment_
- _Find Purpose_
- _Stay Connected_
- _Be an Optimist_

_____

_____

_____

_____

Date: _____ Make Today Count!

CHAPTER 9

WITNESS YOUR THOUGHTS

Courtesy of Maria Napoli

You are in the driver's seat when you listen to your instincts.

Your Mindless Monster—Negative Nudger

Simply noticing is not about understanding or analyzing; it involves paying attention to what's happening right now. When we allow our thoughts to control our experience, we alter that experience. Has this ever happened to you? You are attempting to complete a task. Suddenly you have thoughts that intrude upon your experience that may sound something like "I can't do this. This is too difficult. I failed last time and I know it will happen again." Negative thinking is the central role of our *Mindless Monster* who keeps us stuck in the past or obsessing about the future. Avoiding feelings and thoughts does not solve the problem. If we do not confront those intruding and nudging feelings, thoughts, and behaviors, they are stored and accumulate power, which leaves us feeling more helpless to deal with them. In some respects when we are afraid to challenge those negative feelings, thoughts, and behaviors, we are thrown into the past. Fear prevents us from embracing the present moment. When you think about it, there really is nowhere else to be but right here right now!

Each one of us has a Mindless Monster and some of us have more than one. The role of our Mindless Monster is to keep us in a negative thought process, which prevents us from "being in the moment" and enjoying life to its fullest. How does our Mindless Monster do this? Take Mary, for example. She is an overachieving teacher who usually pushes herself to the point of exhaustion, consequently neglecting herself, feeling tired, and not getting enough rest. Mary's Mindless Monster—let's call it "Want It All Woman"—moves in for the kill when Mary attempts to take care of herself. Her Mindless Monster reminds her to "keep on pushing" and do it all in order to be good enough. Her exhaustion wears down her immune system, making her prone to illness, which, in turn, forces her to slow down. It is unfortunate Mary has to become ill to slow down and take care of herself.

Another example is Jack. He is an easygoing accountant. A devoted father, partner, and employee, he tries to please people and believes that if he gives everyone what he or she wants, they will love and accept him. Needless to say, Jack gives to others but neglects himself. He hopes that others will notice his needs and care for him as he cares for others. When he is not noticed, he feels rejected, angry, and disappointed. Jack's Mindless Monster, the "Purple People Pleaser," reminds Jack he will face rejection if he does not give it all away. He holds on to his resentments and is prone to ulcers and digestive problems.

Our mindlessness traps us in many ways. Here are a few things to consider when evaluating your Mindless Monster:

- Living in the box—you learn one way of doing something and avoid trying new ways of doing the same task.
- Permanent autopilot—you do things without awareness such as brushing your teeth, driving your car, and being stuck in negative relationships.
- Single-mindedness—you hold onto old beliefs and avoid the endless possibilities.

A study of mindfulness and sustainable behavior found that awareness and sustainable behavior were positively correlated and that individuals who were mindful were more likely to pay attention and intentionally process information about environmental impact.[1]

Belinda and Her Dream

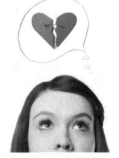

The story of Belinda and her dream is a reminder of how negative thinking can control our relationships. Belinda had been in several romantic relationships that ended in disappointment. She felt that her partners were not interested enough in her, which began a pattern of her making excessive demands for attention. When her partners did not meet her expectations, she became angry and lashed out toward them, all the while feeling rejected. Her last relationship with Derek was the greatest disappointment, as she felt confident that he would be her life partner.

Belinda had a repetitive dream where she feeling content as she walked hand-in-hand with Derek. As the walk continued, thoughts of feeling worthless emerged, setting off a series of accusations toward Derek that he did not love her and in fact desired other women. Belinda awakened from these dreams sweating, feeling angry and anxious with dread of the dream reoccurring. Following the four-step MAC model, Belinda began to make changes.

Through her daily mindfulness practice, Belinda *acknowledged* the excessive demands she placed on Derek for attention and *intentionally paid attention* to her negative self-talk. *Accepting without judgment* her awareness and thoughts for Derek and herself, Belinda began to notice feelings toward her father emerge. She felt angry as she remembered an incident when she placed first in a high school track meet and hoped to receive praise from her father, only to experience his minimizing her success. Memories of feeling unimportant in his eyes brought a deep feeling of sadness. Belinda acknowledged that she was looking for her father's approval and attention in every relationship she encountered, which set the stage for failure. As Belinda let go of her need for approval and attention, she was able to see her relationship with Derek more clearly. When her need for attention reared its head, instead of feeding her unrealistic expectations, she embraced the emotions as a friendly reminder that she was indeed worthy.

 Describe the various ways your Mindless Monster controls you and takes away your personal power.

Describe how it feels.

MAC Your Thoughts

The mind is a beautiful thing! It becomes a danger zone when our thoughts take over the rest of our body, emotions, breath, instincts, and truth. Insomnia is one sign of a mind controlled by thoughts. Insomnia prevails in the lives of millions of people. A racing mind can lead to stress overload and the rationalization of thoughts so that we lose the meaning of the experience. It can be a treacherous road. When repetitive negative thinking is high because of worrying and ruminating, emotional problems have been found.[2] This often leads to disorganization, confusion, and forgetfulness.

College students are faced with many new life style changes such as managing finances and time, cooking, developing new relationships, and the overall challenge of academic life. Students often find themselves staying up late at night. One wonders how that time is actually spent: relaxing or pushing the envelope to get things done? A sleep study of college students evaluating repetitive negative thinking found that students who slept for shorter periods of time and went to bed later experienced more repetitive negative thinking.[3]

How do we enjoy the many thoughts and ideas that we have? Let's look at ways to MAC your thoughts so they serve you instead of throwing you off the path of balance.

Empathically Acknowledge

We all have that little voice inside that sometimes takes us out of the moment without our noticing. That voice can take the form of whispering that we are not good enough or of shouting at us to please others and ignore our own needs. Some have many voices calling out at varying decibels that come in the form of feeling dependent, helpless, entitled, omnipotent, or selfish. Depending upon our life experiences with family, employees, employers, friends, and self, we may have other voices as well. The first step you are learning throughout this book is to acknowledge what the little or big voices are saying. Make friends with your voices and place yourself on top of the power hierarchy. When you take this step, you are able to create the space to move toward the challenge of ultimately quieting your Mindless Monster and engaging your Mindful Captain.

When one views an experience as negative and avoids that experience it affects one's ability to deal with the experience. When avoidance occurs it creates a situation where the attachment to the negative experience amplifies. This contributes to the person's anguish.[4]

Intentional Attention

Pay attention to the many situations you encounter that call out your Mindless Monster. Notice your breathing, muscles, body temperature, and emotions and how they react to those thoughts. Pay attention to the people in your life who may participate in inviting your Mindless Monster to enter a situation. Then realize that when you embrace the moment, your *Mindful Captain* becomes the boss.

Nonjudgmental Acceptance

As noted earlier, we all have those voices that take us out of the moment and throw us into negative thinking. Accept your humanness without judgment and face your Mindless Monster head on instead of ignoring it or running away. When you accept your thoughts, all of them, you give your Mindful Captain permission to accept you, all of you, just as you are.

Willingly Choose

Imagine how wonderful you will feel when your Mindless Monster is asked to leave the premises of your mind! As you open the door for self-acceptance, speaking your truth, and maybe even getting a good night's sleep, you choose to move forward and let go!

Think about your Mindless Monster. You may have several. How does your Mindless Monster invade and control you and prevent you from paying attention to what you need? Once you have reflected and worked on the activities, turn your attention to you Mindful Captain. Witness who you are and who you can become!

Mindful Living

 Mindless Monster: Describe

_____

_____

_____

 Mindless Monster: Describe

_____

_____

_____

Keep a journal of how your Mindless Monster controls you.

 Researchers have found that participants who scored high on avoiding unpleasant thoughts experienced more panic symptoms. Other studies have also found that when one suppresses certain types of thoughts, the number of those thoughts continue to occur, affirming that it is healthier to accept our thoughts as they occur rather than avoid them regardless of what they are.[5]

Draw your Mindless Monster below or use your own paper. Let your instincts and imagination guide your drawing.

What it would be like if you put your Mindless Monster to rest?

Quieting the Mindless Monster

Insomnia is usually a result of your Mindless Monster keeping your thoughts racing when you need to slow down and get ready for sleep. Here is an activity to help you quiet the Mindless Monster when you need to sleep. You must follow these steps exactly as prescribed!

Getting Ready for Sleep

1. Lie down and get comfortable in your bed.
2. Close your eyes.
3. Imagine a blackboard (not a white board) next to you.
4. Imagine a piece of chalk and an eraser on a nearby table.

Let's Sleep

1. Take the chalk and eraser and walk over to the blackboard.
2. Write the number 100.
3. Draw a circle around the number 100.
4. Take the easer and erase everything on the board.
5. Put the chalk and easer back on the table.
6. Pick up the chalk and eraser and go back to the blackboard.
7. Write the number 99.
8. Follow steps 4–6 exactly, counting down until you fall asleep.

The power of the mind goes far beyond our imagination. This simple exercise will remind you of that powerful connection between our physical and mental states.

MINDFUL CAPTAIN—FLEXIBLE FRIEND

As mentioned earlier, "we are all perfect in our imperfections." The impact of experiences from childhood through adulthood often determines the type of Mindless Monster (or Monsters) that we nurture. That little voice is given quite a bit of power when we engage by reacting. There are many ingredients that factor into how we make decisions. If we made rational choices, we might follow classical decision theory, which states that when one makes a decision, the goal is to maximize the gain or expected outcome and use the information of that decision to accomplish that goal.[6]

The problem with this theory is that many of us do not make decisions by weighing the odds of the outcome and taking time to weigh the "checks and balances" of those decisions. Many of the decisions we make are based on how we feel emotionally at the time. If we are feeling emotional about a decision, it may not be a good one.

Let's look at where our Mindful Captain comes in to making good decisions. If we indeed are experiencing emotions when making a decision, those emotions do not have to negatively impact the decision. In fact, when we acknowledge those emotions without judging them, they can be a factor in making a good decision. All the information that is needed to accomplish the goal with a satisfactory outcome increases our ability to choose how we approach the experience. All decisions cannot be based on one way of thinking such as classical decision theory since there are many factors involved in making good decisions for the best outcome. With mindfulness being the key ingredient, we are able to weigh thought, feelings and senses to add to the equation of optimal decision making. Once we acknowledge our Mindless Monster (or Monsters); pay attention to our thoughts, behaviors, and emotions; and accept them without judgment we can then choose to move forward and silence our Mindless Monster(s) with our Mindful Captain.

We know that life will present challenges. Our Mindful Captain is fearless, giving us the courage to move through challenges regardless of the outcome. Mindfully moving through those challenges offers many opportunities for awareness, growth, and the ability to view situations from a new perspective. Time is precious and we know that when we are stuck in old patterns of thinking and behaving we lose those precious moments.

When we engage our Mindful Captain, time is our friend and we push through those negative patterns and are able to embrace new horizons, have a fresh look, and begin building the infrastructure of living in the moment. Regardless of the challenges we face, when we acknowledge, pay attention, and accept without judgment, we are better able to choose how experiences will impact our lives and increase our propensity for happiness. Let's begin empowering your Mindful Captain by reflecting upon your personal inner voices.

Staying focused in the moment is the job of our Mindful Captain. This is the only voice we want to hear and engage while responding to our experiences. Viewing our experiences through the lens of mindfulness will empower us to invite our Mindless Monster to take a back seat. Are you willing to choose to be the Mindful Captain of your ship? If your answer is yes, it is time to stop Taking orders from your Mindless Monster.

What is the role of your Mindful Captain?

Responds

Listens

Takes Risks

Facilitates Guiltless Self Care

Mindful Living

Mindful Captain: Describe

_____

_____

_____

Mindful Captain: Describe

_____

_____

_____

☻ Keep a journal of how your Mindful Captain supports you.

Draw your Mindful Captain below or use your own paper. Let your instincts and imagination guide your drawing.

Describe the various ways your Mindful Captain supports and empowers you.

Describe how it feels when your Mindful Captain supports and empowers you.

Most of us have experienced physical sensations when falling in love, or 'butterflies' in the stomach when feeling happy or anxious. When you complete the follow activity, you will experience how clearly your thoughts impact your behavior.

© Carlos Yudica/Shutterstock.com

Mindful Lemon Imagery

1. Close your eyes.
2. Imagine that you have a bowl filled with lemons cut up in small pieces.
3. Imagine taking one piece and putting it in your mouth.
4. Imagine sucking on the lemon.
5. Notice what happens.

References

1. Amel, E. L., Manning, C. M., & Scott, B. A. (2009). Mindfulness and sustainable behavior: Pondering attention and awareness as means for increasing green behavior. *Ecopsychology, 1*, 14–25.

2. Nolen-Hoeksema, S., Wisco, B.E., & Lyubomirsky, S. (2008). Rethinking rumination. *Perspectives on Psychological Science 3*, 400–424.

3. Nota, J. A., & Coles, M. E. (2015). Duration and time of sleep are associated with repetitive negative thinking. *Cognitive Therapy Research. 39* (2), 253–261.

4. Karekla, M., Forsyth, J. P., & Kelly, M. M. (2004). Emotional avoidance and pathogenic responding to a biological challenge. *Behavior Therapy, 35,* 725–746.

5. Follette, V., Palm, K. M., & Pearson, A. N. (2006). Mindfulness and trauma: Implications for treatment. *Journal of Rational Emotive and Cognitive-Behavior Therapy, 24,* 45–61.

6. Gutnik, L.A., Forogh-Hakimzada, A., Yoskowitz, N. A., & Patel, V. L. (2006). The role of emotion in decision making: A cognitive neuroeconomic approach toward understanding sexual risk behavior. *Journal of Biomedical Informatics 39.* 720–736.

MINDFUL AWARENESS REFLECTION JOURNAL

Choose one mindful experience as you begin your reflection.

Empathically Acknowledge

Describe your experience.

_____

_____

Intentional Attention

Describe what you noticed.

Breath
Body
Emotions
Thoughts
Senses

Accept Without Judgment

Describe judgment; acceptance.

_____

_____

Willingly Choose

Intention/willingness; new perspective.

_____

_____

Mindful Mac Meditation

Describe your meditation experiences. What did you learn from your meditation experience?

_____

_____

Mindful Daily Journal

_____
_____
_____
_____

_____
_____
_____
_____
_____
_____
_____
_____
_____
_____
_____
_____
_____
_____
_____
_____
_____

Tips for Wellbeing

- Have Hope
- Accept Yourself
- Exercise
- Practice Mindfulness
- Express Gratitude
- Master Your Environment
- Find Purpose
- Stay Connected
- Be an Optimist

_____
_____
_____
_____

Date: _____   Make Today Count!

MINDFUL COMMUNICATION

Courtesy of Maria Napoli

Listen to the silence.

MAC Your Communication

When we engage in communication without the impediment of internal or external filters, our connection to the person with whom we are communicating strengthens. There are many styles of communication that are related to one's experience, culture, age, gender, and environment. The most important ingredient to consider is whether or not we are effectively connecting with the listener(s). Regardless of communication style, most of what is communicated is nonverbal. If we stop and think about this, how often are we aware of our facial expressions, body language, physical distance, and tone of speech? We may not be aware of these communicators, yet those we are speaking to are directly impacted by these nonverbal messages. Paying attention to feelings, thoughts, body sensations, and instincts are all nonverbal ingredients that add to mindful communication.

© CartoonStock.com

Non-Verbal Communication

As we have discussed throughout this book, our body is always communicating. What information are we communicating with others? Let's take a look. More often than not, we focus on facial expression when we communicate. There are many other communicators that take an active role and add to a mindful communication interaction. Body language in the form of gestures is an interesting phenomenon in communication. Several studies have found that listener's focus on the speaker's face rather than the gestures being made during a verbal interaction. However, listeners focus on the speaker's gestures more often when 1) the speaker looks at his/her own gestures while speaking, 2) when the gesture is located on the periphery of the speaker's body and in front of the listener's and 3) when the gesture is suspended in midair with a pause before the speaker continues.[1] This example of gesturing while speaking reminds us that our attention to our own body language increases the listener's propensity for focusing not only on our facial expressions but our gestures as well.

Many of us have experienced communicating with someone who speaks a language other than our own. Various attempts at gestures and facial expression can be surprisingly successful. Effectively communicating human emotion through facial expression, even if one does not speak the same language, can happen. In addition to facial expression, does one's tone of voice add to effectively communicating emotion? Does culture factor in how much emotion is communicated? One study found that a speaker's tone of voice was effectively able to communicate emotion regardless of the linguistic similarity. However, in this study, native Argentine speakers were able to recognize emotions more through vocal cues. This result leads to the conclusion that culturally-learned facial and vocal behaviors are recognized and increase communication.[2]

Boys and Girls

From an early age, we begin to see differences between how girls and boys communicate with each other. Boys generally communicate in groups with strong ties, usually in the form of an activity with

well-defined dominance hierarchies. True to what many expect of boys, they generally engage in more physical rough play and when they reach adolescence, they engage in more sports and games than girls do. Boys have been found to talk frequently to each other during their interactions, yet girls have more extensive interactions with their peers. It is not unusual to find girls talking for hours with each other. Think about the average sleepover. Girls often sit up all night talking while boys often sit up all night playing games.

"Okay, let me get this straight; your friend Kristyn is no longer coming to have supper with us because Danielle told you that Tracy heard from Holly that her sister Melissa thought she saw Kristyn in the mall talking to your old boyfriend?"

As girls approach adolescence they share more about themselves than boys do and are more cooperative with each other.[3] Adolescence is a time of increased communication with peers as adolescents are in a place of both physical and emotional transformation. Communicating with others who are experiencing similar changes can be soothing and affirming, yet the pull toward acceptance and competition can derail effective communication with emotional reactions and irrational thinking. Many of the communication patterns that develop for boys and girls continue well into adulthood and color the interactions in friendships, couples, parenting, and the workplace.

"Helen, you're the Team Leader,
why don't you jump first?"

© *CartoonStock.com*

Men and Women in the Workplace

Most of us may agree that there are clear differences in the communication styles between men and women. There is a plethora of information regarding these differences. They have been discussed, accepted, tolerated, and often unchallenged over the decades. As women have fought for equal rights and have taken significant leadership roles in the workforce, communication styles have been examined and the environment of organizations has changed. With regard to sales positions, women have been found to develop the relationship first and then focus on reaching the goal of the sale. Men, on the other hand, tend to be more direct and focus on reaching the goal, building the relationship in the process.[4] One might argue that women have been leaders throughout history and have been striving for recognition and equal rights for centuries. When we look at what is important in life, we realize that being an integral and active participant in relationships is the key, not only to healthy ego development, but happiness as well. Taking this a step further, when we are happy we live healthier lives. One might say that bearing and raising children, managing a household, being a support to partners and family, and over the last few decades, becoming a major player in the workforce places women in key position for leadership. To that end, they have developed a variety of communication skills to be successful leaders.

Although more women are in management positions, African American and Asian American women still comprise only 5.3% and 2.7% of all management positions, respectively.[5] Even though women hold management positions, men still hold significantly more leadership positions. When we look at the differences between how men and women communicate, one might come to the conclusion that women are not strong leaders since their communication style is not dominant. On the other hand, women excel in communication due to their ability to process, explore, and listen. For example, men have been found to use language to enhance social dominance whereas women use language to enhance social relationships. In addition, men tend to offer solutions to problems to avoid unnecessary discussion of interpersonal problems while women use more expressive, polite, and tentative communication.[6] One might perceive that avoiding discussion of interpersonal problems may detract from understanding what is going on and women's tendency to be polite and tentative may be viewed as a weakness in leadership. In general, male leaders may be viewed as "take charge" and female leaders more "take care." [7]

Men and Women Communicating

Let's take a look at two communication experts. John Gray's description of differences in communication styles between men and women from his book *Men Are from Mars, Women Are from Venus: A Practical Guide for Improving Communication and Getting What You Want in a Relationship* has been read by millions of people seeking information on how to effectively communicate to develop intimate relationships. In her book, *You Just Don't Understand: Women and Men in Conversation.* Deborah Tannen also discusses the gender differences in communication styles between men and women, but focuses more on how gender differences begin at a young age.

© CartoonStock.com

"It would never work. I'm from Venus,
you're from Mars."

Gender Communication Differences According To Gray[8]	
MEN	**WOMEN**
Goal-oriented sense of self to achieve results.	Define sense of self by feelings and quality of relationships.
Deal with stress by withdrawing from conversation.	Deal with stress by reaching out and talking.
Deal with conflict by offering a solution.	Deal with conflict by seeking understanding and empathy.

"Inform him I dislike it when
he uses the dog to communicate."

Gender Communication Differences According To Tannen[9]	
MEN	**WOMEN**
Boys create relationships by doing things together.	Girls create relationships by talking.
Converse with the intent to offer information and advice.	Converse with the intent to create rapport and establish and negotiate relationships.
Conversations are negotiations for dominance and power.	Conversations are to negotiate closeness and preserve intimacy.
When men hear women talking, they want to offer a solution, and then dismiss the problem.	Talk about problems with other women fosters a bond and maintains intimacy.

" I DON'T KNOW WHAT IT IS . I THINK
IT'S SOME KIND OF OLD-FASHIONED
CELL PHONE . "

© CartoonStock.com

Children Communicating With Children

© DeepGreen/Shutterstock.com

If you have ever witnessed children playing together, or for that matter, remember your own experiences playing as a child, you will notice how different the communication style of children is from that of adults. Children live in the present. They are spontaneous, creative, and intelligent beings that love adventure. The world is their playground. Children are mindful beings.

Let's read the story of Jack and Jane. It may sound familiar.

Jane comes to Jack's house and taps on the window. She has a big smile on her face. Jack runs to the door without saying a word. There is no plan, simply acknowledging the moment as he joins Jane witnessing the vast world before them. He asks, "Want to play?" She says, "Let's go!" This begins their journey for the day. Together they look around and pay attention to how they feel and what they see. They walk toward the park together. It's a familiar place. At the same time, they see a large mound of sand that stands about six feet tall. This is a new addition. They are not thinking about the purpose of this mound. They run up the mound. Laughing hysterically, they run down, failing to notice their sand-filled shoes. They both look up at the mound. They grab each other's hands, run up to the top, and roll wildly down, feeling the rush of wind and excitement of the unknown.

When they get to the bottom, they are full of sand from head to toe. Looking up at the mound, then the sky, then at each other, they settle down. Jack says, "I'm hungry." Jane reminds him it's her turn to bring a snack. She runs over to her backpack and shares a yogurt, a piece of fruit, nuts, and a bottle of water. Still full of sand, they lick the yogurt off their lips, smell the different scents, and touch the soft fruit as they stir the yogurt around in the cups. When they eat the nuts, both Jack and Jane hold the nuts in their hands and decide to share by evening up the small ones and big ones. They pay attention to their senses while eating and then take a few sips of water. All at once they look at each other, place the empty snack packages in the backpack, and run up the mound once again. This time they discover a new way to play. They find a large piece of cardboard they can both sit on. They drag it up the mound, sit on it together, hold on to each other and slide down, all the while laughing hysterically! After all this excitement, they see some friends playing on the jungle gym. In unison, they run to join them and report the details of their adventure. What a day!

© IrinaK/Shutterstock.com

Parents Communicating With Children

Communication styles between parents and children can set the stage for positive or negative childhood development that impacts children's relationships not only with their parents, but with their future partners, friendships, and eventually their own children. After reading the story about Jack and Jane, adults may not view climbing up and down a sand mound as being as exciting as a child would. What may come to our mind? We might ruminate about the past—"I remember when I fell down and sprained my ankle, this is too dangerous!" We might project into the future—"What a mess, I don't have time for cleaning up all this sand, and the laundry and sand all over the bathtub!" Unfortunately, parents often insulate themselves from the fun and spontaneity of child's play by worrying and projecting negative thoughts. This can create a barrier between parent and child. Short of safety measures, parents may find themselves having more fun if they communicate with their children with mindfulness.

We develop our listening skills early in our own childhood. How we pay attention follows us in all of our relationships. The relationship between parent and child is especially important because prior to the child's development of language skills, parents must develop acute sensitivity to the non-verbal cues that are critical in identifying a child's needs. When parents are not paying attention, the bond that creates trust is decreased, setting the stage for an unhappy child. Parents are given the responsibility to keep children safe from themselves as well as others. The child's cry is only one avenue of communication; body language such as relaxed or stiff muscles, facial expression, tone, and intensity of vocalizations and frequency are all indicators of how children communicate.

SON, YOUR TEACHER TOLD ME THAT YOU'RE HAVING TROUBLE FOCUSING, AND OTHER THINGS THAT I ZONED OUT ON.

12/29   STAHLER.

©Jeff Stahler/Distributed by Universal Uclick for UFS via CartoonStock.com

© CartoonStock.com

As children mature, parents are challenged by their child's independence, which begins at two years old and continues until early adulthood. Other communication styles come into play as the child matures and more often than not, a parent's emotional tolerance is challenged. From the moment a child begins saying "No!" during toddlerhood to "I'm not coming home at that time; everyone else gets to stay out!" parents are challenged. Emotional regulation is often out of balance with parents doing more reacting than responding and moving into fight or flight scenarios. When parents are mindful, they are better equipped to acknowledge their experience as it is happening by empathically "walking in the child's shoes," paying attention to how the child is feeling and behaving, accepting their experience with their child without judgment, and with a compassionate presence. Last but not least, mindful parents choose to live harmoniously in the experience with their child and are able to let go of any negativity that might keep them stuck.

The Mindful Parent

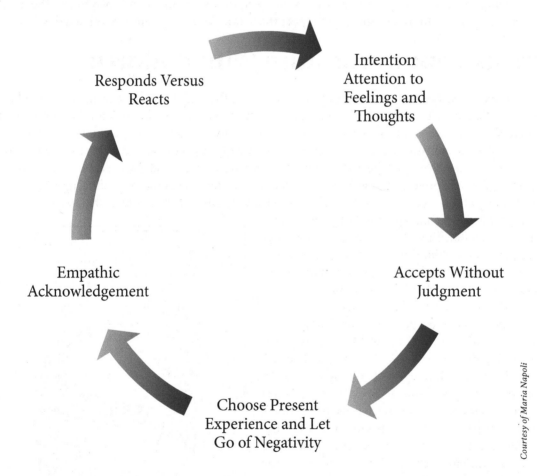

Responds Versus Reacts

Intention Attention to Feelings and Thoughts

Accepts Without Judgment

Choose Present Experience and Let Go of Negativity

Empathic Acknowledgement

Courtesy of Maria Napoli

The mindful parent responds rather than reacts. Acknowledging the experience just as it is without adding internal or external filters; paying attention to all aspects of the experience; letting go of judgment, and choosing to embrace the experience may bring lots of joy and connection between a parent and child. When we think about stories that bring laughter, they are often about spontaneous events that have occurred, or an unexpected outcome. Simply stated, they are about a mindful experience!

Empathically Acknowledge

Paraphrase to let the receiver know that you understand what is being communicated. Use your own words to state what you are hearing. Use the sender's words for clarification.

Tips

- Offer a couple of sentences for every key point the sender makes.
- Try to experience exactly what the sender is communicating.
- If you don't understand, share what you did understand and ask for clarification.

Intentional Attention

Describe your observations of the sender's behavior to clarify what you see feel and hear.

Notice:

- Affect
- Tone of voice
- Rate of speech
- Body language
- Emotions

Example

Mary: I don't have tickets for the concert to see my favorite recording artist. John said he would pick up the tickets, but he forgot. I guess there's always next time.

Paul: It appears to me that you are disappointed that you are not going. Are you upset with John for forgetting?

Mary: No, there's nothing I can do now. (Mary's face tightens. Her voice is restricted and has a low growl to it.)

Paul: I feel that you are upset with John as I see your face tighten and hear some anger in your voice.

Mary: I suppose I am a bit upset with John. I guess I didn't want to admit it. I think I will discuss it with him.

Accept Without Judgment

Before you offer feedback, wait until the sender is finished speaking; then you can give your thoughts, opinions, and feelings without judgment.

Tips

Allow the speaker to finish before you speak.

Accept what was communicated.

Keep the speaker's thoughts and feelings in mind when responding.

Willingly Choose

When we own our experience and make "I" statements, we take responsibility for our actions, words, and behavior, which enhances our ability to communicate mindfully.

A study explored the impact of mindfulness-based training on working memory capacity and affective experience in two military groups preparing for deployment to Iraq. The soldiers who practiced mindfulness demonstrated improvement more frequently over time compared to the control group. The more they practiced, the more working memory capacity increased.[10]

Listen to the Silence

People often do not want our opinions or advice; they simply want to be heard. Be mindful of sharing a loving presence when words are not necessary.

Choose a time during the week when you can observe silence for a few hours. Turn off the cell phone, television, IPod, and any verbal communication. Describe your experience.

Courtesy of Maria Napoli

_____

_____

_____

_____

_____

_____

_____

_____

The Filly and Her Mother

A beautiful filly lived with her mother in the countryside. The grassy fields were filled for miles with wildflowers. Her mother was a critical horse who prided herself in the thought that her opinions were indeed fact. The filly often felt she ignored her own thoughts and desires to avoid her mother's judgment. One spring day, the filly watched the rain fall for hours over the fields while her mother slept soundly. When her mother woke, she said to the filly, "Go and get us some hay to eat. I'm hungry!" The filly responded, "Mother, the mud is too deep near the haystack from the rain. We should wait until it dries a bit. It could be dangerous." Her mother whinnied, "You lazy child, I'll go myself to eat and you will have to stay hungry." She galloped through the wet grass, laughing at the stupidity of her filly that stayed behind. When she got closer to the haystack, she began to sink into the mud. As she struggled to climb out, she wailed, "Help me, my beautiful filly." This time the filly did not listen to her mother and instead waited for the mud to dry. When she finally went out to help, her mother cried, "My beautiful filly, what can I do to please you for rescuing me from this horrible situation?" The filly looked at her and said, "Instead of criticizing and judging me, listen to me, for I am wise, too."

Mindful lesson: When we listen instead of judge, we create opportunity instead of obstacles.

Communication Styles

Passive Communication *Is* Withdrawing

- Do not say what we want.
- Let others make decisions.
- Feel resentful and expect people to know what we want.
- Say "yes" when we mean "no."
- People-please instead of self-please.
- Avoid challenges to avoid failure.
- Feel isolated because we fear intimacy.
- Disconnect.

© JrCasas/Shutterstock.com

"Don and I rarely fight. Then again, we rarely talk."

© CartoonStock.com

Aggressive Communication *Is* Reactive

- Don't own our feelings, and blame, accuse, and threaten others.
- Appear to know more than others.
- Push our opinions on others.
- Often feel angry and want control.
- Hurt and humiliate others to get what we want.
- Often feel anxious and tense.

© CartoonStock.com

Assertive Communication Is Responsive

- Take responsibility for our feelings and actions using "I" statements.
- Empathically listen and respond.
- Clear in identifying our needs while respecting others.
- In control and confident without pushing ourselves onto others.
- Make contact with others in a respectful and caring manner.

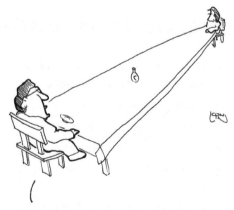

MARGARET, I FEEL THAT WE MUST TALK ABOUT OUR RELATIONSHIP.

Communication

Finites keep us blindfolded. Words like *never* and *always* cloud reality and leave little room for process and discussion. The fact is few things in life are finite.

Dictators are words that move us into places we don't want to go. Words like *should, must, ought to,* and *have to* often elicit resentment. Imagine if we eliminated these words from our vocabulary. We might just begin enjoying life more and embrace each situation rather experiencing it as a burden.

- Never
- Must
- Should
- Have to
- Always
- Ought to

The Buddhist teacher Thich Nhat Hanh tells a story about Allen, a man who enjoyed spending time doing things he wanted. He felt he had carved out quality time for himself. When Allen married, he felt slighted at times because he had to divide his time between doing what he wanted and what he now felt obligated to do. When Allen and his wife had a child, he felt his private time was divided once again. He struggled with these "new dictators" of should's and have to's. Allen finally realized that if he changed his attitude and embraced his new life and the changes that accompanied it, there were no dictators. He began to see his time with his wife and child as joyous moments for himself instead of seeing them as something he had to give up.[13]

When we change our attitudes and perceptions, we begin to enjoy life more fully.

"If workers listen to each other with presence and pay close attention, we may minimize misunderstanding and confusion, which may reduce mindless time and energy spent repairing what we did not understand because 'we were not really paying attention.' Guide to mindful listening: Bring attention to breath and body, listen to your worker, and stay with the breath without interrupting."[12]

References

1. Gullberg, M., & Kita, S. (2009). Attention to speech-accompanying gestures; eye movements and information uptake. *Journal of Nonverbal Behavior 33,* 251–277. doi 10.1007/s10919-009-0073-2

2. Pell, M. C., Monetta, L., Paulmann, S., & Kotz, S. A. (2009). Recognizing emotions in foreign language. *Journal of Nonverbal Behavior, June 33* (2), 107–129.

3. Rose, A. J., & Rudolph, K. D. (2006). A review of sex differences in peer relationship processes: Potential trade-offs for the emotional and behavioral development of girls and boys. *Psychological Bulletin* 131 *January,* 98–131. doi:10.1037/0033-2909.132.1.98

4. McQuiston, D. H., & Morris, K. A. (2009). Gender differences in communication: Implications for salespeople. *Journal of Selling and Major Account Management Vol 9,* 54–64.

5. Bureau of Labor Statistics. (2012). Unpublished Tabulations from the 2010 Current Population Survey, "Table 1: Employed and Experienced Unemployed Persons by Detailed Occupation, Sex, Race, and Hispanic or Latino Ethnicity," Annual Averages 2010.

6. Basow, S. A., & Rubenfeld, K. (2003). "Troubles talk": Effects of gender and gender typing. *Sex Roles,* 48(3/4),183–187.

7. Martell, R. F., & DeSmet, A. L. (2001). Gender stereotyping in the managerial ranks: A Bayesian approach to measuring beliefs about the leadership abilities of male and female managers. *Journal of Applied Psychology, 86,* 1223–1231.

8. Gray, J. (1992). *Men are from Mars, Women are from Venus: A practical guide forimproving communication and getting what you want in a relationship.* New York: HarperCollins.

9. Tannen, D. (1990). *You just don't understand: Women and men in conversation.* New York: Ballantine Books.

10. Roemer, L., Litz, B., Orsillo, S., & Wagner, A. (2001). A preliminary investigation of the roles of strategic withholding of emotions in PTSD. *Journal of Traumatic Stress, 14*(1), 149–156.

11. Barnes, S., Brown, M. K. W., Krusemark, E., Campbell, W. K., & Rogge, R. D. (2007). The role of mindfulness in romantic relationship satisfaction and responses to relationship stress. *Journal of Marital and Family therapy, 33*(4), 482–500.

12. Ucok, O. (2006). Transparency, communication and mindfulness. *Journal of Management Development, 25*(10), 1024–1028.

13. Hanh, T. N. (1976). *The miracle of mindfulness: An introduction to the practice of meditation.* Boston: Beacon Press.

MINDFUL AWARENESS REFLECTION JOURNAL

Choose one mindful experience as you begin your reflection.

Empathically Acknowledge

Describe your experience.

_____

_____

_____

Intentional Attention

Describe what you noticed.

Breath
Body
Emotions
Thoughts
Senses

Accept Without Judgment

Describe judgment; acceptance.

_____

_____

_____

Willingly Choose

Intention/willingness; new perspective.

_____

_____

_____

Mindful Mac Meditation

Describe your meditation experiences. What did you learn from your meditation experience?

_____

_____

_____

Mindful Daily Journal

TODAY'S Insight

Tips for Wellbeing

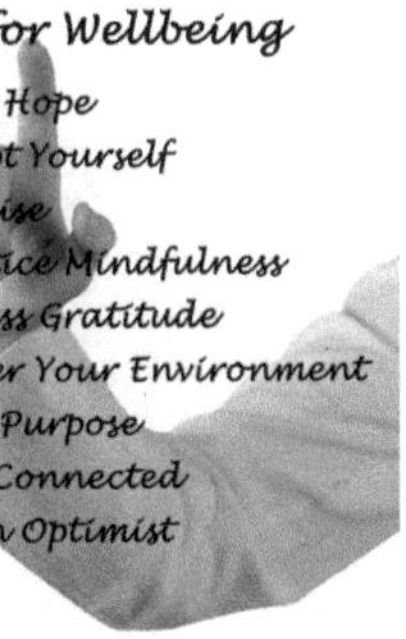

- Have Hope
- Accept Yourself
- Exercise
- Practice Mindfulness
- Express Gratitude
- Master Your Environment
- Find Purpose
- Stay Connected
- Be an Optimist

Date: _____ Make Today Count!